NEGOTIATING
flexibility

*The role of the social
partners and the State*

NEGOTIATING
flexibility

The role of the social partners and the State

General editor **Muneto Ozaki**

INTERNATIONAL LABOUR OFFICE • GENEVA

Ozaki, M. (ed.)
Negotiating flexibility: The role of the social partners and the State
Geneva, International Labour Office, 1999
/Labour flexibility/, /Collective bargaining/, /Trade union role/, /Employers organization/, State intervention/, /Developed country/, /Developing country/. 13.01.2

ISBN 92-2-110865-1

ILO Cataloguing in Publication Data

Printed and Bound in Great Britain by Biddles Ltd, Guildford and King's Lynn

CONTENTS

LIST OF ACRONYMS

ACTU	Australian Council of Trade Unions
AF	Federation of Norwegian Professional Associations
AFL-CIO	American Federation of Labor and Congress of Industrial Organizations
AIRC	Australian Industrial Relations Committee
AFSCME	American Federation of State, County and Municipal Employees
ANPE	Public Employment Agency (France)
ATW	Working Time Act (the Netherlands)
AW	Labour Act (the Netherlands)
CAW	Canadian Autoworkers
CFDT	French Democratic Confederation of Labour
CFTC	French Confederation of Christian Workers
CGC	French Confederation of Executive Staffs
CGT	General Confederation of Labour (Argentina and France)
CNPF	National Council of French Employers
COLA	cost-of-living allowance/adjustment
CPI	consumer price index
CUPE	Canadian Union of Public Employees
DGB	German Confederation of Trade Unions
DOLE	Department of Labor and Employment (the Philippines)
EC	European Commission
EU	European Union
FKTU	Federation of Korean Trade Unions
FNV	Netherlands Trade Union Confederation

FO	Force Ouvrière (France)
FTC	fixed-term contract
GDP	gross domestic product
IAM	International Association of Machinists
IBEC	Irish Business and Employers' Confederation
ICTU	Irish Congress of Trade Unions
JIT	just-in-time
KCTU	Korean Confederation of Trade Unions
LMC	labour-management council
LO	Norwegian Confederation of Trade Unions
LO	Swedish Trade Union Confederation
NHO	Confederation of Norwegian Business and Industry
OECD	Organisation for Economic Co-operation and Development
OJT	on-the-job-training
ÖTV	public sector union (Germany)
PNR	Programme for National Recovery (Ireland)
PRP	performance-related pay
QPE	Quality, Precise delivery and Economy
QWL	quality of working life
RSU	works council (Italy)
SAF	Swedish Employers' Confederation
SEIU	Service Employees International Union (United States and Canada)
SIPTU	Services, Industrial, Professional and Technical Union (Ireland)
SMATA	Union of Engineering and Related Workers in Motor Transport (Argentina)
TCO	Swedish Confederation of Professional Employees
TPM	total productive maintenance
TQM	total quality management
TUC	Trades Union Congress (United Kingdom)
UAW	United Autoworkers (United States)
UFCW	United Food and Commercial Workers' Union (Canada)
USWA	United Steelworkers of America
VF	Engineering Employers' Federation (Sweden)

INTRODUCTION

Economic globalization and technological innovation are now exposing enter-prises, which used to be sheltered by national borders and national institutions, to harsh competitive pressures (ILO, 1997, p. 83). The competitiveness of an enterprise or economy in the globalized market depends largely on its ability to adapt to changes in markets and to take advantage of the latest technological innovations. It is widely believed that, to enhance this ability, the labour market must be made more flexible. As higher competitiveness and the consequent economic growth facilitate – but do not automatically result in – job creation, employers and many policy makers see the formation of flexible labour markets as the key to solving the persistently high levels of unemployment in many parts of the world. Accordingly, changes are being introduced into labour markets worldwide at an accelerating pace, with a view to enhancing their flexibility.

This book discusses the extent to which the labour market is becoming more flexible, as well as the role which collective bargaining is playing, or can play, in the process of introducing this flexibility. For this purpose, collective bargaining is understood in its widest meaning, including bipartite and tripartite negotiations at the national, sectoral, enterprise and shop-floor levels. The information contained in this book has been largely drawn from 22 country studies specifically prepared in 1997 for this project, covering both industrialized and developing countries across Western Europe, North and South America, and Asia.[1] Several

---

[1] Argentina: Oscar Ermida Uriarte; Australia: Nick Wailes and Russell D. Lansbury; Belgium: Alfred Pankert; Brazil: Oscar Ermida Uriarte; Canada: Peggy Kelly; France: Youcef Ghellab; Germany: Reihard Bispinck; India: C.S. Venkata Ratnam; Ireland: Joseph Wallace and Noreen Clifford; Italy: Marco Biagi; Japan: Motohiro Morishima; the Republic of Korea: Chang-Hee Lee; the Netherlands: Ben Dankbaar, Lei Delsen and Willem de Nijs; New Zealand: Anthony Honeybone; Norway: Bjørne Grimsrud and Torgeir Aarvaag Stokke; Peru: María Luz Vega Ruiz., the Philippines: Rosalinda Dimapilis Baldoz; Spain: Patricia Torres and María Luz Vega Ruiz; Sweden: Birger Viklund; United Kingdom: James Arrowsmith, Mark Gilman and Keith Sisson; United States: Peggy Kelly; and Venezuela: María Luz Vega Ruiz. As these studies are the primary source materials for this book, in most instances the information drawn from them will not be referenced explicitly.

of these studies will be available as working papers on the ILO's Labour Law and Labour Relations Branch website.[2]

The study focuses on the role of collective bargaining in negotiating labour market flexibility. It does not seek to ascertain quantitatively the effects of flexibility on competitiveness, employment or other macroeconomic indicators. This issue has been a central focus of concern for policy makers over the last decade, and has been the subject of considerable, and still inconclusive, debate. Arguments which have been popular among some media and academic circles, contrasting the "successful" neo-liberal models of the United States and the United Kingdom against an "over-regulated" European social market, appear less and less convincing in the face of growing evidence revealing the complexities of this relationship. For example, some recent evidence shows that strict employment protection legislation, as well as legislation on such labour market standards as working time, fixed-term contracts, minimum wages and employees' representation rights, do not have any serious implications for average levels of unemployment (Nickell, 1997). Recent evidence also demonstrates that coordinated collective bargaining – whether at a higher or decentralized level – is more conducive to high economic performance than uncoordinated decentralized collective bargaining (Traxler and Kittel, 1997). So rather than seeking further quantifiable evidence supporting any particular point of view on this issue, this book focuses on the perception and behaviour of the social partners with respect to labour market flexibility.

Labour market flexibility here refers to the ability of an enterprise (i) to adjust the level and timing of labour inputs to changes in demand, (ii) to vary the level of wages according to productivity and ability to pay, and (iii) to deploy workers between tasks to meet changes in demand. An enterprise's ability to achieve these objectives is normally enhanced by introducing changes in contracts of employment, working time, pay systems and work organization. Accordingly, the study focuses on recent changes taking place in these four aspects of the employment relationship. They are among the factors making up "external numerical flexibility", "internal numerical flexibility", "wage flexibility" and "functional flexibility", concepts frequently used in academic debates on labour market flexibility.

To reiterate, we are *not* assuming that all the changes introduced into these four aspects of the employment relationship necessarily lead to higher efficiency – let alone a reduction in unemployment. The book nevertheless reports any evidence we may have come across on the specific relationship between flexibilization and economic performance.

---

[2] http://www.ilo.org/public/english/80relpro/index.htm

Collective bargaining has been playing a significant (although not always a prominent) role in bringing about these substantive changes in the employment relationship. If well conducted, it remains the most effective means of striking the optimal balance between economic efficiency and the protection of workers' interests. Moreover, the participatory nature of collective bargaining has the capacity to enrol workers' support in the drive for greater flexibility. However, collective bargaining itself has undergone a transformation in many countries, as the flexibilization of labour markets has made headway. In many cases, the introduction of measures aimed at making the labour market more flexible has often been accompanied, or facilitated, by changes in the procedures for regulating the employment relationship. For example, decentralizing industrial relations, in particular collective bargaining, is regarded by many employers and observers as a precondition for successfully enhancing labour market flexibility. In those countries where labour market rigidities lie mainly in excessive legislative regulation, a greater role entrusted to the social partners in regulating the labour market, or greater freedom for individual employers and workers in shaping their reciprocal relationship, tends to be conceived as a means of enhancing flexibility. Accordingly, this book also examines the changes under way in industrial relations, in particular the changing role of the State, as well as the level at which collective bargaining is carried out. It also seeks to highlight any shifts taking place in the respective weights of various means of regulating the labour market, such as legislation, collective bargaining, individual contracts of employment and unilateral employers' decisions.

Chapter 1 analyses the types and extent of flexibility that have recently been introduced in the labour markets of the countries studied. The relative importance of various means of introducing labour market flexibility, such as legislative reforms, collective bargaining, individual contracts of employment and unilateral employers' decisions is explored in Chapter 2. Chapter 3 looks at the extent to which the role of the State in industrial relations, and the level at which collective bargaining takes place, have undergone changes or have remained stable in the process of spreading labour market flexibility. Chapter 4 reviews the positions of employers and trade unions on labour market flexibility, as well as any changes – particularly among trade unions – that have recently taken place in their positions. The outcomes of negotiations on flexibility, including bipartite and tripartite negotiations at the central, sectoral and enterprise levels, are the focus of Chapter 5. In the concluding chapter, we discuss the contributions which collective bargaining can make to labour market flexibility, as well as the factors that enhance the effectiveness of collective bargaining as a means of introducing such flexibility.

This book is a result of teamwork among members of the ILO's Labour Law and Labour Relations Branch. The following were primarily responsible for the drafting: Youcef Ghellab, Anthony Honeybone, Peggy Kelly, Chang-Hee Lee, Andrés Marinakis, Alfred Pankert, Zafar Shaheed and Anne Trebilcock. Other members of the branch were also involved in preparing the book, particularly Malcolm Crotty, Mary Hamouda, Nicolas Laniel and María Luz Vega Ruiz. Muneto Ozaki was responsible for coordinating the different chapters and Peggy Kelly edited the manuscript.

TYPES OF FLEXIBILITY 1

Introduction

The notion of making the labour market more flexible is not a new phenomenon. Employers, for their part, have long sought to introduce greater flexibility into work practices. As far back as 1964, for example, Alan Flanders wrote about the "Fawley productivity agreements" which transformed the work organization and pay policies of a British oil and gas refinery. Two primary features characterized these agreements. The first was a productivity package deal, where the company agreed to provide pay increases of up to 40 per cent in exchange for the unions' assenting to changes in work practices. Such changes included relaxing job demarcations, redeploying workers, and adding temporary and permanent shift working. The second feature was a major scaling back of the use of systematic overtime, which had reached a peak of 18 per cent of total hours worked.

Decades later, we are observing negotiations which touch upon many of these same kinds of changes. The difference today, however, is the pace at which flexibility agreements are being reached. Flanders noted that the Fawley agreements "were without precedent or even proximate parallel in the history of collective bargaining in Great Britain", if not the world (Flanders, 1964, p.13). But what was once a rare occurrence has become an increasing popular trend.

This chapter will attempt to describe and quantify, to the extent possible, the acceleration of this trend towards greater flexibility in the labour market, with a focus on developments in the 1990s. Four areas will be reviewed and examined separately: contracts of employment; pay; working time; and work organization.

Contracts of employment

One widespread method of enhancing flexibility in the labour market has been the introduction of changes in regulating employment contracts. More concretely, it has taken the form of relaxing controls over (i) recourse to what have come to be commonly referred to as "atypical" employment contracts, and (ii) termination of employment contracts at the initiative of the employer.

Neo-classical economists argue that legal requirements moderating the use of atypical contracts of employment and the recourse to termination of employment have negative effects on employment. These controls tend to discourage employers from hiring new employees because they impede the adaptation of the volume of labour to fluctuations in demand. Although as yet no conclusive empirical evidence seems to support this argument, there is today a widespread perception – among government officials, employers and an increasing number of trade unions – that the relaxation of legal controls over contracts of employment is an essential element of increased flexibility in the labour market. It is illustrative that the reduction of legal requirements, over both the recourse to atypical employment contracts and the termination of employment, has been the main feature of the labour law reform agenda of numerous governments in the last decade.[1]

Flexible employment

By flexible employment, we refer to any form of employment which is not full-time employment for an indefinite duration. It is sometimes called atypical employment (de Grip et al., 1997; Delsen, 1995), contingent employment (Belous, 1989) or precarious employment (Treu, 1992), although there are often differences in the precise definitions given by various authors to these different terms.

The following forms of employment constitute the main types of flexible employment, although the precise legal definitions given to each of them vary widely from one country to another:

- part-time employment: any employment for less than the national standard working week;
- temporary work: any employment for a fixed period or fixed piece of work, including work arranged through temporary work agencies;
- casual employment: employment of an irregular or intermittent nature;

---

[1] The spread of flexible employment to sectors of economic activity other than agriculture, commerce and construction was hampered for a long time by legal constraints in many countries. In particular, the traditional labour law precepts in civil law countries required that all employment relationships should be established for an indefinite period of time. Fixed-term contracts were permitted only when the duration of the employment relationship was limited by the nature of the work involved. Upon the completion of the work, or at the end of the stipulated period of time, the contracts were terminated automatically. Since the early 1980s, however, fixed-term contracts, without specifying the work to be accomplished, started spreading among industrialized countries in the context of the worsening economic crisis. The continuous development of such contracts until now has resulted in their constituting one of the main forms of employment, and has led to the questioning by some observers of the basic principle that employment should be stable.

- employment under training contracts: a combination of training and employment, including apprenticeship; and
- seasonal employment: intermittent employment at a specific time of the year.

While the last four categories all illustrate types of "precarious employment" (i.e. jobs that do not involve a long-term, uninterrupted employer-employee relationship), part-time employment may or may not be carried out under the same terms and conditions as traditionally "standard" or "regular" forms of employment (albeit with proportional reductions in wages and certain benefits to reflect the fewer number of hours worked). Thus the treatment of part-time work in law and in collective agreements ranges from placing it on an equal footing with full-time work to excluding it completely from many forms of protection.

In addition to the forms of flexible employment mentioned above, recourse to outsourcing or subcontracting is spreading fast as an instrument for enhancing labour market flexibility. Although contracting out does not involve an employment relationship strictly speaking, it may accomplish the same function as flexible employment by providing employers with an alternative to standard, full-time, open-ended employment.

The spread of flexible employment

Flexible employment has grown over the past two decades in most countries covered in this study. This is illustrated by a significant fall in the share of the standard workforce (defined as full-time employees without a limit on the duration of their employment) in the total labour force, although the importance of the fall varies widely from one country to another. For example, in Australia, the standard workforce fell from 67 to 57 per cent of all workers between 1982 and 1995, while over the same time period full-time and part-time casual employment doubled, currently accounting for about 25 per cent of all employed persons (Australia country study). In the United Kingdom, 38 per cent of employed persons were reported to be working on a non-permanent, non-full-time basis in 1993 (IRS, 1994, pp. 5–6). Statistical data on developing and newly industrializing countries are scarce, and those available are not necessarily comparable internationally. In the Philippines, according to a survey carried out by the Department of Labor and Employment (DOLE), the percentage of workers employed under flexible labour contracts[2] reached 14.2 per cent in 1994 (15.7 per cent in 1992), up from 13.7 per cent in 1989 (the Philippines country study). The results of another survey conducted by DOLE in collaboration with the ILO in 1990 showed that 64 per cent

---

[2] This expression covers part-time, casual and contract workers.

7

of the firms surveyed reported employing, or otherwise using the services of, workers under flexible labour contracts.

Public services have by no means remained immune to such developments. In France, flexibilization has mainly taken the form of subcontracting (e.g. catering in trains, schools and hospitals, as well as prison supervision). In Italy, a government legislative decree (No 29/1993) implementing Act No 421/1992 privatized the employment relationship for public employees (with the exception of such categories of public servants as diplomats, magistrates, prefects, armed forces, police and university professors) by providing that it should be regulated through individual contracts and collective agreements.

In the public sector of the United Kingdom, the percentage of temporary employees (defined as employees under contracts of one year or less) grew from 35 per cent to 45 per cent between 1984 and 1990. One striking feature is that the flexibilization of employment contracts in the public sector preceded the rapid spread in the 1990s of flexible employment in the private sector. This phenomenon of the public sector temporarily overtaking the private sector on the way towards flexible employment can also be observed in New Zealand, where the encouragement given by the State Sector Act of 1988 resulted in a much lower level of full-time permanent employment in the public sector (66 per cent) than in the private sector (79 per cent) in 1991. By 1995, however, the private sector had caught up with the public sector, the proportions having become 69 per cent and 68 per cent, respectively (Brosnan and Walsh, 1996, cited in the New Zealand country study). These are examples of the private sector following the trends set by the public sector, which had reformed its employment system in an imagined vision of the private sector. In flexibility debates, perception – and not reality – may sometimes be the determinant of people's behaviour.

Let us now analyse, in some detail, the spread of the two most widespread forms of flexible employment aimed at enhancing numerical flexibility: part-time employment and temporary employment. Table 1.1 shows recent trends in their prevalence in selected countries of the Organisation for Economic Co-operation and Development (OECD).

The table highlights two noteworthy trends for the period 1985 to 1995. First, the proportion of part-time workers to the total number of employed workers has increased in 11 countries (Australia, Belgium, Canada, France, Germany, Ireland, Japan, the Netherlands, New Zealand, Spain and the United Kingdom), out of 14 countries for which data are available. In some countries, such as Ireland and the Netherlands, the proportion of part-time workers increased dramatically from 1985 to 1995, by 86 per cent and 65 per cent, respectively. Second, the proportion of temporary workers has increased in eight countries (Australia, Canada, France, Ireland, the Netherlands, Spain, Sweden and the United States), out of 12 countries

Table 1.1. Evolution of part-time and temporary workers as a percentage of total employment in selected OECD countries, 1985, 1990 and 1995

Country	Part-time work			Temporary work		
	1985	1990	1995	1985	1990	1995
Australia[1]	17.5[a]	21.3	24.8	15.6[e]	18.7	23.5[e]
Belgium[2]	8.6	10.9	13.6	6.9	5.3	5.3
Canada[1]	16.8[b]	17.0	18.6		7.5[d]	8.8[e]
France[2]	10.9	11.9	15.6	4.7	10.5	12.3
Germany[2]	12.8	15.2	16.3	10.0	10.5	10.4
Ireland[2]	6.5	8.1	12.1	7.3	8.5	10.2
Japan[1]	15.8[b]	18.8	19.8	10.3	11.0	10.4[e]
Netherlands[2]	22.7	31.8	37.4	7.5	7.6	11.4
New Zealand[1]	15.3[b]	20.0	21.5	—	—	—
Norway[1]	29.6	26.3	26.5	—	—	14.0
Spain[2]	5.8[a]	5.0	7.5	15.6[a]	29.8	35.0
Sweden[2]	25.7[a]	23.8	25.8	11.9[a]	10.0	12.5
United Kingdom[2]	21.2	21.7	24.1	7.0	5.1	7.0
United States[1]	18.4[b]	16.9	18.6	—	0.8[d]	2.2[e]

— data not available.

[1] OECD, 1996–97. [2] European Commission, DG V, 1996, pp.147–162.

[a] 1987 data; [b] 1983 data; [c] 1984 data; [d] 1989 data; [e] 1994 data.

for which data are available. In some countries the growth observed was exponential: for example, France (+162 per cent) and Spain (+124 per cent). In the Netherlands, two-thirds of the country's employment growth was in part-time jobs between 1987 and 1994, while between 1994 and 1996, 40 per cent of the new jobs created were flexible jobs, such as fixed-term, on-call and temporary agency work (the Netherlands country study). In France, an analysis of the structure of the 2 million jobs on offer collected by the Public Employment Agency (ANPE) in 1995 showed that only 35 per cent of them were for an indefinite period. The remaining 64 per cent consisted of the following: 33 per cent for a fixed term (1 to 6 months); 19 per cent for a fixed term (> 7 months); and 12 per cent for temporary work through agencies.

The trends shown in table 1.1, particularly for Western Europe, are corroborated by a recent survey carried out by the European Commission (EC), which shows that between 1991 and 1994 the majority of jobs created were on a part-time basis. This was the case for both men and women. The trend continued in 1995 when, of all new jobs created, 71 per cent of those for men and 85 per cent of those for women were part time. Moreover, a considerable proportion of the jobs created in 1995 were fixed term. In fact, temporary work represented the whole share of the increase in male employment and almost half that of female employment in the European Union (EU). More than 50 per cent of the unemployed who found jobs in 1995 had to accept temporary work (EC, 1996, pp. 18, 53–54).

The relative importance of different forms of flexible employment

The overall picture of the evolution of flexible employment painted earlier should not hide the fact that the prevalence of specific forms of flexibility differs from country to country. Here we examine differences among countries in the relative importance of part-time versus temporary work, and other forms of external numerical flexibility such as casual work and seasonal employment.

Generally speaking, three types of approach can be identified:

(i) countries where the emphasis is much more on external numerical flexibility (temporary work, as well as contract and non-regular work) than on internal numerical flexibility (part-time work);

(ii) countries where the emphasis appears much more on internal numerical flexibility than on external numerical flexibility; and

(iii) countries where there seems to be a relatively balanced use of these two forms of numerical flexibility.

The first group of countries includes Italy, the Philippines and Spain. These countries have experienced a greater development of subcontracting (Italy), temporary and casual work (Philippines), and temporary work (Spain) than part-time work.

In Italy, firms primarily resort to manpower flexibility through subcontracting. Indeed, such a strategy of external numerical flexibility seems to be confirmed by the very large percentage of self-employed workers in total employment (24.5 per cent in 1995), the highest among the EU Member States (EC, 1996, p. 155). This reportedly took the form of micro-enterprises largely set up by former employees of big industrial companies (Kaisergruber et al., 1997, p. 107). Between 1993 and 1995 the number of independent workers increased by 1.6 per cent, while that of salaried employees dropped by 0.1 per cent, further signifying a trend towards externalization of production (ibid.).

In the Philippines, the share of part-time workers in non-agricultural activities is very low (below 1 per cent in all economic sectors except community, social and personal services), while the share of casual workers is much higher. The movement towards casual work has been facilitated by the existence of a large labour surplus, composed mostly of young workers (15 to 24 years of age) with little training, education and skills (the Philippines country study). Thus, a large majority of temporary and casual workers are in low-paid, low-skilled positions for which replacements are easy to find.

In Spain, the proportion of temporary work as a percentage of total employment appears quite high (29.8 per cent in 1990 and 35.0 per cent in 1995). By contrast, that of part-time work is among the lowest in the OECD (5.0 per cent in 1990 and 7.5 per cent in 1995) (EC, 1996). The very high prevalence of temporary employment seems largely due to the legal framework in place until 1997 which permitted recourse to it under a wider range of circumstances than in other countries (although the situation has since changed, as the social partners agreed to relax the regulation on termination of employment contracts for an indefinite duration as a means of reducing the unusually high amount of temporary employment). The limited recourse to part-time employment, however, may be due to the lack of incentives for employers to resort to part-time workers, as these workers are entitled to the same benefits as full-time workers. This is in contrast to the situation prevailing in the United States, for example, where part-time workers are often paid less than full-time workers, thus making their employment financially attractive to employers.

The second group of countries includes Germany, Japan, the Netherlands, Norway, Sweden and the United States. In these countries, companies resort much more to part-time employment than to temporary employment (see table 1.1). Although the reasons for relatively limited recourse to temporary employment may differ from one country to another, a feature common to many of them is a high level of internal labour market flexibility. This is particularly so in Japan, the Netherlands, Norway and Sweden. High internal labour market flexibility reduces the need to resort to temporary workers as a means of adjusting the volume of the workforce to fluctuations in demand (Delsen, 1995, p. 84).

The United States also has an insignificant proportion of temporary employment (2.2 per cent in 1995), which may seem surprising for a country that is considered to have one of the more flexible labour markets in the world. However, as there are very few restrictions on termination of employment in general in the United States, employers may not feel a strong need to resort to temporary employment. On the other hand, the high percentage of part-time work may be partly accounted for by the fact that part-time workers are frequently paid less than full-time workers: according to Delsen (1995, p. 23), the hourly wage rates for part-time workers in the United States are often 15 to 20 per cent lower than those for comparable full-time workers. Part-timers are also far less likely to receive fringe benefits such as health insurance, pensions and paid annual leave – which also produces major cost savings for employers.

The other countries in this group have a higher percentage of temporary employment among total employment than the United States, such as Norway with 14 per cent. Fixed-term contracts represent the main form of temporary work in Norway. They are most common in the public sector, and of less importance in the private manufacturing industry. Resort to temporary work is still quite limited, despite the fact that the number of temporary work agencies registered by the Ministry of Labour jumped from 95 in 1994 to 170 in 1996. The total activity handled through temporary work agencies is estimated to represent 0.5 per cent of all work in Norway (Norway country study). However, the regulation of temporary work has been tightened in that country since February 1995, and this may represent a shift in the Government's policy towards encouraging firms to choose forms of flexibility other than temporary work.

The third group of countries includes Australia, France and Ireland, where firms appear to resort as much to temporary work as to part-time work. As table 1.1 shows, in 1995, the percentage of part-time work and temporary work among total employment comprised, respectively, 24.8 and 23.5 per cent[3] (Australia), 15.6 and 12.3 per cent (France), and 12.1 and 10.2 per cent (Ireland). This is not to confuse the fact, however, that temporary and part-time work have two different functions in the labour market, and their respective spread, or decline, emanate from different causes.

Changes in the prevalence of temporary employment often reflect changes in the regulations on termination of employment. In Australia, for example, recourse to temporary employment accelerated following the tightening up of regulations on termination of employment introduced by the Industrial Relations Reform Act of 1993, which restricted employers' ability to terminate the employment relationship. As a large majority (70 per cent) of part-time workers in Australia are hired on a temporary basis, trends in the prevalence of part-time work largely coincide with those for temporary workers.

In France, cost saving has no doubt played a role in the development of part-time work. Under an Act Nº 92-1446 of 1992 (*"relative à l'emploi au développement du travail à temps partiel et à l'assurance chomage"*), employers who create new jobs on a part-time basis or convert existing full-time jobs into part-time ones, while maintaining the volume of hours, are granted a 50 per cent reduction in their social security contributions. This figure was reduced to 30 per cent in 1993, reflecting the Government's concern for alleviating the burden on the national budget. Such legislative encouragement aimed at creating employment may have boosted the growth of part-time jobs. As to the growth of temporary work in France, the available evidence indicates that it is at least partly due to the relaxation, since 1986, of the legal framework governing the recourse to temporary work, and the growing tendency among some enterprises to use fixed-term

---

[3] Data for 1994.

contracts as a means of making selections among potential permanent staff (Michon and Ramaux, 1992).

Gender, age and flexible employment

As table 1.2 indicates, the prevalence of part-time employment varies significantly according to sex, with women far more likely than men to be engaged in this form of flexible employment. A closer look at the data, however, foretells a reversal of this trend. In 13 of the 15 countries examined, there has been a greater increase in the rate of part-time employment among men than among women from 1990 to 1996. The difference is quite dramatic in certain countries, such as Norway and Sweden, where the rate of part-time employment actually declined for women over this period, while it rose 17 per cent and 24 per cent, respectively, for men. These figures may help to explain recent evidence suggesting that a significant percentage of part-time workers in most countries are in such employment involuntarily. In 1995, the percentage of involuntary part-timers among the total number of part-timers was 41 per cent in Canada (Statistics Canada, 1992-95), 39 per cent in France, 33 per cent in Ireland, 39 per cent in Italy, and 35 per cent in Sweden (Eurostat, 1996). More men than women in particular are working part time, not out of choice, but because they cannot find full-time jobs.

The available data also suggest that temporary employment is more prevalent among young workers than other age groups. According to a recent OECD study, workers under 25 years of age are far more likely to be employed under fixed-term contracts than older workers. In 1994, the probability of a worker in the 20-24 age group being employed under a fixed-term contract was 35 per cent, 23 per cent and 71 per cent in France, Germany and Spain respectively, while for a worker aged 25 or over it was 8 per cent, 6 per cent and 27 per cent, respectively. Such a finding is not surprising, as non-standard employment contracts, in particular temporary employment contracts, have become the normal mode of entry into the labour market for young workers (Treu, 1992, p. 503).

Regulation of termination of employment

Legal regulation of the termination of contracts of employment can be regarded as inhibiting flexibility by limiting the employer's power to dismiss "at will", thereby acting as a brake on the ability to achieve external numerical flexibility. This is why a number of countries have taken steps to loosen the regulatory and administrative controls placed on termination of employment. Among the more important ways in which countries have relaxed legal controls over dismissals

Table 1.2. Distribution of part-time employment, male and female, in selected
OECD countries, 1990 and 1996

Country	Women employed part-time as % of all women employed		Men employed part-time as % of all men employed	
	1990	1996	1990	1996
Australia[2]	40.1	42.	8.0	11.7
Belgium[1]	25.8	30.5	2.0	3.0
Canada[2]	26.8	28.9	9.1	10.7
France[1]	23.6	29.5	3.3	5.3
Germany[1]	33.8	33.9[a]	2.6	3.6[a]
Ireland[1]	17.7	22.1	3.4	5.0
Italy[1]	9.6	12.7	2.4	3.1
Japan[2]	32.8	36.0	9.3	11.5
Netherlands[1]	59.4	66.1	15.0	16.1
New Zealand[2]	35.0	37.3	8.4	10.4
Norway[2]	47.5	45.7	8.6	10.1
Spain[1]	12.1	17.0	1.6	3.1
Sweden[1]	41.5	39.0	7.5	9.3
United Kingdom[1]	43.2	42.7	5.3	5.6
United States[2]	25.2	26.9	10.1	10.9

[a] 1995 data.

Source: [1] European Commission, 1996. [2] OECD, *Employment Outlook*, 1997.

is by broadening the scope of exclusions from unfair dismissal legislation –
commonly to exclude flexible forms of employment. Countries have also eased
or abolished administrative controls, such as trade union consultation requirements or prior governmental approval, in order to simplify dismissal procedures
for employers.

Relaxing legal controls on termination can be considered as one way of
achieving enhanced employment flexibility. Particularly if combined with relaxing
legal controls on the use of flexible forms of employment, it may also be expected
to have contributed to an increase in external numerical flexibility in those
countries in which such relaxation has occurred. However, this enhanced
flexibility has been achieved at the cost of a corresponding reduction in security
of employment for employees.

Flexibility in employment and job tenure

The growing recourse to flexible forms of employment and relaxing the regulation of termination of employment contracts have had effects on stability of

employment in some countries. For example, between 1985 and 1991, the percentage of workers with less than one year's seniority increased in the Netherlands and Spain respectively by 105 per cent and 57 per cent. However, in the countries studied as a whole, the effects of changes in forms of employment and in regulating dismissals on the rate of labour turnover seem to have been relatively minor. Even in the Netherlands and Spain, workers' average job tenure in a particular enterprise decreased only moderately in the same period, from 8.9 years to 7 years and from 11.2 to 9.8 years, respectively.

Changes in average job tenure of workers cannot be exclusively attributed to flexible employment or changes in regulating dismissals. Average tenure may be influenced by a complex set of other factors (OECD, 1993), including the gender, age and education of the workforce, as well as human resources development and training policies adopted by enterprises. Nevertheless, the data on job tenure enable us to make rough evaluations of the importance of the effects of the changes in forms of employment and in regulating dismissals on the stability of employment.

In most industrialized countries, a high level of job tenure has prevailed since the 1960s. In fact, 1993 data confirmed the widespread practice of long-term employment in nine OECD countries, with even a small increase evident in the tenure of older workers, particularly in Japan and, to a lesser extent, Germany. By contrast, a clear erosion of long-term employment has taken place in the United Kingdom and the United States with respect to male workers over 50 years old. A slight reduction was also apparent (except for Japan) in average job tenure for workers in their twenties (Marsden, 1996).

These data seem to suggest that the prevalence of the neo-liberal model of free hiring and firing may be a myth that requires cautious evaluation. Employers in many countries have argued that the possibility to terminate employment easily and at low cost was a prerequisite for recruiting new employees. Legislators and policy makers in a number of countries have heeded the employers' plea, and promoted flexible employment and relaxed the regulation of termination of employment. However, not all employers appear to be taking advantage of the new possibilities afforded to them as, after all, flexibility in employment alone does not automatically lead to higher productivity. Employers are also increasingly recognizing the limits to the advantages they can draw from recourse to non-standard employment contracts or from frequent recourse to dismissals. This trend may be illustrated by a decision made in 1996 by Ford Motor Company in the United States to limit the number of its contingent workers to no more than 10 to 15 per cent of the total workforce, after realizing that such workers can be a hindrance in operations that demand a flexible, well-trained workforce. Contingent workers may save the company money in the short run, but their poor skills and lack of experience can prove quite costly in the longer term. This leads us to doubt whether, in spite of its ranking high on the agenda of labour market reforms in many countries today, the flexibilization of employment contracts – apart from the growing recourse to contract labour – will continue to be pursued as a principal means of enhancing labour market flexibility in the decades to come.

Pay flexibility

Pay flexibility, which employers and governments are today seeking to enhance throughout the world, is in essence the responsiveness of wages to changes in individual and collective productivity, and to competitive cost pressures exerted by markets. The current debates among policy makers, employers, trade unions and researchers are focused on the following aspects of pay determination: systems of wage bargaining; minimum wages; linking pay to performance; and wage indexation.

Discussions of wage bargaining tend to focus on the level at which bargaining takes place. Some believe that wage bargaining at the centralized or branch level may create difficulties for lower-productivity enterprises, whereas bargaining at the enterprise level can take better account of the particular conditions of the firm. These arguments will be further explored in Chapter 3, along with a full discussion of recent changes in bargaining structures. As to minimum wages, it is often claimed that they constitute an obstacle to job creation, in particular for young and lower-skilled applicants for jobs in the formal sector, as they impede employers from recruiting workers at the lowest wage scales. Linking pay to performance is viewed as a means of motivating workers and improving the overall productivity of the enterprise. Finally, wage indexing is considered to reduce the responsiveness of the labour market to changes in labour supply and demand by creating downward rigidity of real wages.

Therefore, the search – mainly by governments and employers – for greater flexibility in pay determination has tended towards decentralizing wage bargaining (in both the private and public sectors), weakening the real level of minimum wages or abolishing minimum wages altogether, strengthening the link between pay and performance, and attenuating the link between wages and prices. This section will examine the trends in three of these areas, while the topic of wage decentralization will be handled in Chapter 3.

The changing role and perceptions of the minimum wage

The minimum wage has also been at the centre of debates over labour market flexibility, largely due to the widespread perception that it could "price out" less skilled workers from the labour market and exert upward pressures on average wages, thereby fostering inflationary trends. Thus, the minimum wage, which was created as an instrument for alleviating poverty, has come to be regarded by some as an obstacle to economic performance. Various measures have therefore been taken recently, in a number of countries, with a view to reducing the effects of the minimum wage. These range from abolishing the minimum wage to eroding its effects through freezes imposed on it or the absence of periodical adjustments. There are also cases in which special lower rates of minimum wages have been established for specific categories of workers, such as young people.

The United Kingdom probably provides the most drastic example of flexibilization in this respect, as the minimum wage determination system itself was abolished in 1993, leading to a considerable lowering of wages for vulnerable categories of workers. The Labour Government elected in 1997 has decided to restore minimum wage fixing, but in such a way that minimum wages would not affect average wages.

The United States adopted a softer approach to achieving downward wage flexibility, simply by failing to enact legislative adjustments to the federal minimum wage, thus allowing it to fall significantly in real terms during the 1980s and the early 1990s. Opponents of an increase in the minimum wage argued that it would force thousands of employers to lay off workers, and that the teenage unemployment rate would soar. These fears have proved unwarranted, as six months after the 1996 increase in the minimum wage 2 million jobs had been added to the American economy and the unemployment rate had dipped below 5 per cent – one of the lowest levels in decades.

In the Netherlands, in response to a sharp increase in the unemployment rate in the late 1970s and early 1980s, the minimum wage was reduced by 3 per cent in 1984 and then frozen until 1990. Furthermore, in 1992, the way the minimum wage was linked to increases in average wage growth, which had been restored during 1990 and 1991, was modified in accordance with what is commonly referred to as the "Indexing Act". Under this Act the minimum wage will be linked to increases in average wages only if the burden of taxes and social security does not exceed a certain threshold.

Reflecting a widespread concern that the minimum wage might restrict access to the labour market for those vulnerable people for whom it was created as an instrument of social protection, efforts have been made in some countries to lower the minimum wage rate for certain specific groups of workers. In Norway, for example, the Government adopted a so-called youth guarantee for people under 25 years of age in 1995 who are in jobs for training purposes. These jobs, which can be in either private or public enterprises, pay less than the minimum wages agreed upon in different collective agreements. Furthermore, following a reform of the upper secondary school system in 1995, the wage level for apprentices was reduced from about 70–80 per cent to 50 per cent of a skilled worker's wage rate. This was accepted by the unions in return for a major increase in the number of apprentices. Other countries, including Belgium, some provinces of Canada, France, Luxembourg, the Netherlands, New Zealand, Portugal and Spain have implemented similar youth sub-minimum wage rates.

Although the merits of minimum wage fixing are questioned in many countries in the context of the arduous search for better economic performance, other countries have recently introduced, or are on the verge of introducing, a minimum wage. This is the case of the Republic of Korea, which established a tripartite system of minimum wage fixing in 1987 at a time when many countries were questioning their own wage systems. The Korean system was instituted as part of a broad move towards greater democracy and participation by workers in sharing the fruits of economic development to which they had contributed. It was also conceived as a means of reducing what had been perceived as excessive intervention of market forces in pay determination. The practice, however, has been neither smooth nor easy, and the negotiations within the National Wage Council for fixing minimum wages have been laborious, mainly due to the lack of trust between employers and workers arising from the legacy of the era of repressed labour rights.

A closer analysis of the impact of minimum wages in several countries leads us to question the widespread perception that the minimum wage per se constitutes an obstacle to wage flexibility. Evidence indicates that during the period when the Conservative Government in the United Kingdom abolished the minimum-wage fixing machinery, greater wage flexibility was achieved through decentralizing of pay bargaining than through abolishing minimum wages. In New Zealand, statistical evidence for the period 1984 to 1990 (i.e. before the promulgation of the Employment Contracts Act of 1991, which extensively deregulated the labour market) shows that the pay determination system, underpinned by a national minimum wage and condemned as excessively rigid by the proponents of the 1991 labour market deregulation, was in fact delivering considerable pay flexibility through the formal award system, and many of the wage increases of the period resulted from voluntary discretionary payments by employers (Harbridge and Rea, 1992, cited in the New Zealand country study). In the Republic of Korea, between 1988 and 1994, following the establishment of minimum-wage fixing machinery, the minimum wage increased rapidly in real terms, but slightly declined as a percentage of the average wage (in 1994, it was 32 per cent of the average wage). Since then, adjustments in nominal minimum wages have roughly followed the trend in labour productivity.

These examples seem to show that establishing a minimum wage does not necessarily constitute an obstacle to enhancing pay flexibility. Much seems to depend on the level at which the minimum wage is fixed, the context in which the system is introduced and applied, and whether there are special provisions made for certain groups of workers.

Linking pay to performance

The current pressures for higher competitiveness have incited a growing number of enterprises to establish new linkages – as opposed to traditional piece-work systems, whose use continues to decline – between the pay of specific workers or groups of workers and their performance. The concern now is to promote factors of performance other than simple output, such as quality, cost reduction and adaptability. There has also been a recognition that group effort needs to be promoted, rather than simply relying on and rewarding individual effort. Consequently, pay systems in more and more enterprises are today designed and administered so as to link pay more directly than in the past to the firm's financial performance (through profit-sharing schemes), productivity or other specific operational aspects of the enterprise (through gain-sharing plans), or workers' skills (through competency payments).

Profit sharing and gain sharing usually incorporate a variable component in pay, which is linked to some indicator of performance. In the case of profit-sharing schemes, the indicator will be the profit of the enterprise or business unit. For gain-sharing schemes, performance will be measured through productivity, quality, cost cutting, or other factors that affect the efficiency of the firms' operations. In the case of competency payments, as workers acquire new skills in accordance with pre-established criteria, enterprises incorporate an additional payment on the understanding that these new skills will improve workers' overall performance.

Trends in the practice of performance-related pay (PRP) (a catch-all term referring to all systems linking pay to performance) point to several factors that may influence its prevalence. One such factor concerns the effectiveness of trade union activities at the enterprise level and at higher levels. PRP tends to be less widespread in countries such as the Netherlands, Norway and Sweden, where union density has traditionally been high, workers' representation within the enterprise is effective, and the collective bargaining machinery has wide coverage. Another factor that may affect the prevalence of PRP is the encouragement given by the State through legislation or fiscal incentives (for details, see Vaughan-Whitehead, 1995). This has been the case in France, the United Kingdom and the United States, where the data seem to indicate a growth in employees covered by such schemes after the introduction of legislation or fiscal incentives. The third factor is employers' attitudes. Employers may find this PRP attractive, as it is not normally regarded as part of the wage and, therefore, is not subject to social security contributions. However, the high administrative costs involved, difficulties in measuring performance and the high probability of bonuses persisting even when performance no longer warrants them can discourage employers from implementing PRP. In the Netherlands, for example, employees' share ownership and profit sharing have not made significant inroads despite government encouragement through fiscal incentives.

An additional factor influencing the prevalence – and the success – of PRP is the extent to which it is agreed to, and negotiated with, workers. Many case studies have shown that PRP is more likely to succeed if workers are periodically involved in a review process and are consulted on both the performance measures and the rewards for performance. Communication, consultation and devolution of responsibility have also been shown to play a prominent part in the success of PRP.

In France, PRP is generally regarded as one of the main instruments for achieving wage flexibility, covering more than 30 per cent of private sector employees. In this country, where only 20 per cent of workers are covered by enterprise-level collective agreements, the Government has encouraged the practice of PRP through successive legislation and fiscal incentives. As a result, workers' participation in the firm's growth[4] has spread dramatically in recent years. From 1986 to 1994, the number of such agreements increased nearly fourfold, from 2,630 to 8,612, while the number of workers covered more than doubled, from 1,113,709 to 2,513,073 (Ministry of Labour).

The United Kingdom, in the context of declining union power, decreasing coverage of collective bargaining, and government encouragement in the form of fiscal incentives, has witnessed an even faster spread of PRP, particularly in the number of employees covered by profit-related pay schemes since the late 1980s. It is notable that the percentage of PRP in total pay is higher in the United Kingdom than in France. The United States has also had significant experience with PRP – generally called "contingent" or "alternative" pay systems. In 1995, one-third of workers under collective agreements covering 5,000 workers or more were included in provisions enabling them to receive additional compensation from contingent pay arrangements. Moreover, a 1996–97 compensation planning survey of over 2,500 employers found that 15 per cent of them were operating gain-sharing plans, and an additional 11 per cent said they were considering the introduction of gain sharing. This is a sharp rise from 1993, when only 9 per cent of employers offered such plans.

In Australia, as a result of the encouragement given by the federal Government and the arbitration body (Australian Industrial Relations Commission) through the

---

[4] "Participation in the firm's growth" (*participation aux fruits de l'expansion*) refers to deferred profit-sharing that, under a 1967 law, is compulsory for all companies with over 50 employees – "deferred" refers to the fact that employees can withdraw cash from the profit-sharing fund only after a period of five years.

transformation of the National Wage Cases, 16 per cent of collective agreements in 1994 provided for future wage increases based upon productivity; 11 per cent had specific performance pay provisions, while 4 per cent provided for gain sharing. In New Zealand, a 1995 survey of collective agreements revealed that only 7 per cent of workers were covered by productivity arrangements in 1993/94 (Harbridge and Honeybone, 1995, cited in the New Zealand country study). However, a 1996 survey of 562 employers showed that 44 per cent reported an increased use of performance-based remuneration, while 13 per cent were not sure, 41 per cent reported no change, and only 2 per cent said the practice had been reduced (NZIER, 1996).

In Italy, a 1993 national tripartite agreement gave an impetus to the spread of PRP. The agreement provides that "pay increases agreed upon by company bargaining are to be closely linked to the results achieved in terms of productivity, quality and other elements of company-level competitiveness". According to a survey carried out in 1996, 53 firms out of the 104 investigated resorted to performance pay. Big companies seem most interested in this form of flexible pay, as only two of the 12 firms surveyed with more than 5,000 employees stated that they did not have any collective form of variable pay, compared to one-third of firms with between 1,000 and 5,000 employees and half those with between 500 and 1,000 employees (Italy country study).

By contrast, only 1 per cent of enterprises in Canada had productivity bonuses and profit-sharing schemes in 1980 and again in the early 1990s, while the percentage of collective agreements providing for such schemes actually decreased from 14 per cent in 1980 to 8 per cent in 1992. This may be partly due to union resistance to compensation schemes that stress individualized pay rates and link pay increases to outcomes (e.g. profits) that are considered to lie outside the control of workers. In Norway, where union density and the coverage of collective bargaining are both high, only 10 to 15 per cent of private sector employees claim to receive some kind of PRP. In the Netherlands, despite the Government's encouragement of profit sharing and share-ownership through fiscal incentives, these two forms of flexible pay – particularly the latter – remain a marginal phenomenon. Indeed, only 4 per cent of enterprises with more than 10 employees have some form of share-ownership, covering 125,000 employees, a majority of whom are managerial and senior staff. Profit sharing is more widespread. It concerns 27 per cent of the enterprises with more than 10 employees, and covers 500,000 workers; the average amount of profit-related pay represents 6.5 per cent of the gross salary (the Netherlands country study). As mentioned earlier, the relatively limited spread of PRP in the Netherlands seems to have been largely due to the reluctance of some employers to use it; in order to avoid the difficulties involved in operating PRP, some Dutch employers seem to prefer the use of multi-skilling, instead of performance, as a criterion for additional rewards.

We now turn our attention to the countries in Latin America and Asia. Until recently, pay flexibility in Latin America was a macro-level issue, with wage adjustments following more or less periodical, and more or less formal indexation. Given the very high rates of inflation, even when pay was adjusted to 100 per cent of past inflation every month, real wages in fact remained flexible. Over the past few years, however, the approach of policy makers in the region to remuneration issues has changed. The new significance of labour costs in open economies seeking stabilization has made the total pay package more important than simply the basic wage. As a consequence, PRP has begun attracting growing interest.

It must be noted, however, that profit sharing is not new in Latin America, as countries such as Chile, the Dominican Republic, Mexico, Peru and Venezuela have long ago incorporated such schemes in their legislation. Yet a recent experiment in Brazil, where the Government promulgated a provisional measure[5] in 1994 providing that all enterprises should bargain a profit- sharing or gain-sharing scheme with their workers, introduced several innovative aspects into the region. First, it offers the possibility of opting for gain sharing instead of profit sharing. Thus workers may opt for a scheme linking pay to one or more variables that are relevant to improving particular aspects of company performance (for example productivity, quality of products, reducing rework or use of inputs) rather than merely the financial success of the firm. Therefore, the measure has the potential of linking pay to organizational improvements. Second, it does not impose any particular scheme or percentage, but only the obligation for the social partners to bargain. Neither does it determine the level at which this negotiation should take place. While some agreements have taken place at the sectoral level, it seems evident that the spirit of the law is to encourage collective bargaining at the enterprise level.

In Argentina, changes have been less notable in recent years than in Brazil. In the absence of any supporting legislation for fostering the development of profit sharing, its practice is very limited in Argentina. Some recently established large multinationals (for example, General Motors, Chrysler and Toyota) are experimenting with gain-sharing schemes, but these schemes are virtually absent from older established firms. In general, the use of variable pay systems is very rare and traditional extra elements of remuneration (such as seniority, family allowance, low absenteeism bonus, etc.) still predominate in collective agreements.

Flexible pay is also a significant phenomenon in some Asian countries. In Singapore, for example, the flexible wage system has been implemented since

---

[5] Provisional measures are issued by the executive for matters considered to be of great importance and urgency. Their validity is for one month, but the Government can reissue them if Congress has not dealt with the subject in the meantime. This provisional measure has been reissued every month with some modifications.

1986, in accordance with the principle that wage increases should reflect economic performance. As a result, part of the remuneration follows the movement of the firm's results, with the variable wage component today representing 15.9 per cent of total annual salary. In Japan, the tax and social security systems encourage firms to resort to flexible pay, leading to a substantial part of remuneration being paid in the form of bonuses.

Turning now to the public service, where PRP is sometimes referred to as "merit pay", there is typically a greater emphasis on the performance of individual workers. Canada was one of the first countries to set up a system linking pay to performance in the public service, and has been applying this system to senior officials and management since 1964. In the early 1980s, a lump-sum system was extended to other public employees as well, particularly the professional and scientific categories. The United Kingdom began implementing PRP in the public service in the mid-1980s. The system initially targeted managers, but was progressively extended to all staff categories. It comprises a bonus, which is revised annually, and may either consist of additional performance-related increments on top of the normal base pay or a discretionary movement within a pay-band in a given grade. In the public service of Sweden, pay is increasingly linked to work effort, resulting in growing differences in the pace of wage increases among different groups of public employees.

A number of countries have attempted to apply the kinds of individual performance systems which prevail in the public service to the private sector as well. However, the scope of such flexible pay remains somewhat limited. In France, for example, individualization of pay has been mostly confined to large enterprises and to managers. According to the Ministry of Labour, 29 per cent of managers received only individual increments in 1993, against 13 per cent among blue-collar workers. A similar kind of segmentation is apparent in the United Kingdom. According to a 1997 survey, variable pay represented 20 per cent of the total pay of senior executives, compared to just 4 per cent and 5 per cent of total pay for clerical and production workers, respectively (Towers Perrin, 1997). The introduction of PRP among lower-category (and lower-income) employees is difficult, because performance is often outside their control.

Overall, PRP has had mixed results. It has proved effective in countries implementing stabilization programmes, for example, as it has worked as an escape valve for employers in response to pressures for higher wages. Variable pay schemes such as lump-sum payments have enabled employers to agree to additional remuneration, but as only a one-time, non-cumulative element – thus avoiding wage inflation. Yet in other countries, PRP has been somewhat proble-matic. In the Republic of Korea, for example, individualized forms of PRP are now on the decline, partly in response to union pressure. Employers, too, became disenchanted with the practice, as bonuses tended to become a fixed element of pay and lost all links with performance. Indeed, a recent Korean survey revealed that almost 80 per cent of establishments did not reflect the results of personal assessment in determining the amount of bonuses.

Despite the positive and negative characteristics of PRP, there has been a significant increase in the number of workers covered by such schemes. However, the effect on workers' total remuneration has remained somewhat limited. The percentage of the workers' pay linked to performance (including profit sharing) is normally low, and does not exceed 6–7 per cent.

In all cases, it is necessary to deal with various practical problems that tend to characterize variable pay. Foremost among these are issues related to the extent to which (i) workers have a say in the design, implementation and revision of pay systems, and (ii) other human resource management practices are combined judiciously with variable pay in seeking to motivate workers.

Attenuating or breaking the link between wages and prices

Breaking the link between wages and prices has been at the top of the wage flexibilization agenda in many countries. The case of the Netherlands has been mentioned with reference to the minimum wage. Italy abandoned its complex indexation system of the *scala mobile* in 1993. Wage indexation, when established at the macro level without taking into consideration other features of the enterprise situation, is perceived as imposing rigidity in the wage-determination process. What is in question is how automatic are the adjustments and the extent to which indexation can be applied across the whole economy. However, it is generally accepted that the evolution of prices is a critical element that the social partners are bound to take into account in wage negotiations.

In developing countries with a fair degree of government intervention in pay adjustments, the cost-of-living allowance or adjustment (COLA) has been a key feature of pay increases. In India, for example, COLA or "dearness allowance" has become a perennial element of workers' acquired rights in government-enforced pay adjustments. However, exceptions have been provided for under the Sick Industrial Companies Act of 1985, where the dearness allowance may be linked to productivity rather than movements in the consumer price index (CPI), or frozen for limited periods of time, to give the "sick company" a better chance to recover. A bicycle manufacturing concern in Madras tried the first option, which is rather exceptional, for two years. However, after the industry's profitability improved, the union was able to renegotiate linking the allowance with the CPI again. Some enterprises, particularly those in the public sector, take the step from freezing dearness allowances to freezing wage adjustments altogether. For instance, in the 1993-95 round of wage negotiations for 240 public sector enterprises under the central government, 25 per cent of them gave no pay increase. Since most collective agreements had expired at the end of 1991, the pay freeze had in fact lasted even longer.

The highly formal system of wage indexation that for many years characterized wage determination in Brazil has undergone a major change as a result of a dramatic stabilization programme, called the "Real Plan", implemented since late 1994. A key element of the programme consisted of eliminating any formal wage indexation, and confining wage policy to the determination of the minimum wage. However, because of the sharp fall in the inflation rate (to 9.1 per cent in 1996) that resulted from implementing the stabilization programme, workers were better off in terms of purchasing power than they had been in the preceding period marked by high inflation and wage indexation.

In certain industrialized countries with decentralized bargaining structures, a favoured means of maintaining purchasing power has been negotiating COLAs in collective agreements, although there has been considerable erosion of this means of income protection in recent years. In Canada, for example, COLAs became popular in the 1950s and were quite commonly used by the 1970s as a means for dealing with inflation. As inflation began to decline in the early 1980s, COLAs were no longer triggered (i.e. inflation failed to reach the level at which they would become payable). This made it easier for employers in some cases to remove the COLA clause during subsequent bargaining rounds. In 1981, 30 per cent of collective agreements in Canada had COLA clauses; by 1993, this proportion was down to 17 per cent. And in the majority of cases where they were retained, COLAs did not generate an adjustment in wages.

A similar decline is evident in the United States. During the inflationary period of 1975–84, 60 per cent of workers under major collective agreements were covered by COLAs. As inflation moderated in the late 1980s, however, COLAs were traded against other more pressing concerns, such as health-care benefits, pensions and job security. Thus by 1995, only 16 per cent of workers under major collective agreements (22 per cent of private sector workers and 6 per cent of state and local government employees) in the United States were covered by COLAs. Interestingly, however, COLAs have remained popular in the manufacturing sector, covering 57 per cent of such workers.

These examples show that, although prices remain an important factor to be taken into account in wage determination, the automatic indexation of wages to prices has lost much of its importance. As the process of pay determination has become decentralized, the main criteria of pay determination have become enterprise specific (such as productivity or efficiency) or person specific (such as individual performance), with the goal of moderating the inflation rate.

Working-time flexibility

Traditional working time consisted of full-time work for a specified number of hours per day (e.g. eight) and a specified number of days per week (e.g. five). Times for starting and finishing work, breaks and periods of minimum daily rest were all pre-determined, and all workers in a defined group were placed on the same schedule. This pattern has come to be regarded as increasingly unsatisfactory by many employers and workers. In a growing number of countries, therefore, various experiments have recently been made with new types of working-time arrangements. In France, for example, flexible working time has been the cornerstone of the successive initiatives for enhancing labour market flexibility taken by the Government since the 1980s.

The direct causes of modifications in working-time arrangements vary. In some cases, the new flexible working time is a means of reducing, if not eliminating, overtime pay. In others, it is a concession which workers make as a condition for employers' acceptance of shorter working time. Most frequently, however, it is conceived as a means of enhancing the ability of the enterprise to respond, quickly and at low cost, to the accelerating fluctuations in demands for goods and services emanating from the customer.

Working-time flexibility is not new. In most countries covered by this study, arrangements such as shift work, night work and work on Sunday have existed for a long time, although they were confined to specific occupations and sectors such as hotels and restaurants, health services, and some manufacturing industries. The difference today is the spread of working-time flexibility across varied groups of workers and activities and the many forms it has taken – ranging from annualization of working time, to extended closing hours of shops and public services, shorter working weeks and more flexible leave provisions.

Annualization of working time

"Annualization" refers to the practice of calculating the weekly working time on a yearly basis, thereby enabling working time to vary from one week to another. A key characteristic of annualized hours is that there is no overtime payment as long as the total hours worked throughout the year do not exceed a prescribed limit. Of course, enterprises should still observe the existing limitations on maximum working hours per day and per week. In order to make annualization of working time more attractive to workers, it is often combined with a reduction in total working hours, as has been the case in France, Italy, the Netherlands, Spain and the United Kingdom.

The United Kingdom has extensively experimented with annualized hours, especially in those industries where demand is variable and unpredictable, as well as in continuous process industries. This has facilitated the introduction of 12-hour shifts, weekend-only shifts and seven-day weeks, without incurring the costs of overtime pay (the quid pro quo has been shorter working weeks or shorter days). One consequence of the extensive annualization of working time is that there are more workers in the United Kingdom working over 48 hours per week than in any other EU country, especially in transport and communications.

In France, Act No 93-1313/1993 (*"relative au travail, à l'emploi et à la formation professionnelle"*) introduced the possibility of fluctuating weekly working time over part or the whole of the year, within a defined limit, provided this is accompanied by a reduction in working time. Since then, an increasing number of manufacturing enterprises have tended to calculate working time, including part-time work, on a yearly basis in order to adapt to variations in demand. In Italy, a number of industry-level collective agreements provide a framework for annualized hours, including part-time work. In the textile industry, for example, a 1995 national agreement allowed textile firms to deal with variations in production needs by establishing different work schedules at particular times of the year, while limiting total overtime to 96 hours per worker per year. Workers may be asked to work over 40 hours, but not more than 48 hours a week, during periods of intensive production demand, while they may work fewer than 40 hours per week during slower periods. The workers receive the same weekly pay during both long and short weeks, thereby circumventing overtime pay. In the Netherlands, where working hours are also calculated on an annual basis, many agreements have combined longer working days (nine hours per day) with shorter working weeks (four days per week). As a result, the average length of the working week has declined.

Even where there is no visible national trend towards annualization of working time, there are important, albeit isolated examples of this practice. In the motor industry in Argentina, for instance, annualized hours were fixed at newly established companies at greenfield sites such as Chrysler, General Motors and Toyota (2,080 hours, 2,138 hours and 2,133 hours respectively), often through collective agreements negotiated before the opening of the factories. On the other hand, long-established companies such as Fiat have retained the traditional methods of calculating working time. In Spain, a collective agreement at Alcatel Cable Iberica has introduced annualized working time by allowing longer weeks during the second half of the year, when a higher level of demand for products is expected.

The limits imposed by legislation on the possibility of annualizing working hours are more stringent in some countries than in others. In Norway, for example, the averaging of working hours over a period not exceeding one year is allowed through written agreement between the social partners; however, it may be extended over a period longer than a year only with the permission of the labour inspectorate. In any event, working hours may not exceed 48 in any one week, and daily hours may not exceed nine hours (Norway country study). By contrast, annualized hours are prohibited for non-salaried workers in the United States, as working-time legislation requires the payment of overtime for any hours worked in excess of 40 per week, even if working hours are reduced in subsequent weeks.

Innovations in daily and weekly working hours

The organization of daily and weekly working hours has also been made considerably more flexible in an increasing number of countries. In many cases, this has been achieved through legislative changes authorizing the social partners to agree upon innovative working-time arrangements. Legislative restrictions on weekend work have also been relaxed in many countries. Flexibilization of daily and weekly working hours is normally geared to enhancing the ability of the enterprise to fully exploit its operational capacity, by extending hours of operation, and strengthening management control over the timing of labour input.

Australia and New Zealand have gone very far along the road to flexible working hours. The majority of workers in Australia are today employed on a non-standard working week, with only 37 per cent of the total labour force working a 40-hour week: 32 per cent work more than 40 hours and 25 per cent work fewer than 40 hours per week. A survey carried out in February 1995 indicated that 70 per cent of enterprise agreements contained provisions on flexible working hours. Of these, 66 per cent provided for increased flexibility in starting and finishing times, 21 per cent had changes to make the days off provided under the industrial awards more flexible, 20 per cent provided for taking breaks and mealtimes in a more flexible manner in order to avoid interruptions to production, and 15 per cent provided alterations to shift-work provisions (Australia country study).

In New Zealand, there has recently been an increase in the percentage of workers working on Saturdays and Sundays as part of the normal working week. As far as workers covered by collective agreements on working time are concerned, the proportion increased from 30 per cent in 1992–93 to 41 per cent in 1994–95 (Harbridge and Crawford, 1997, cited in the New Zealand country study). In such sectors as hotels and restaurants, retail trade, agriculture, finance, community services, health and mining, more than 80 per cent of workers were covered by such arrangements. This was largely due to removing the definition of an "ordinary working week" through the enactment of the 1991 Employment Contracts Act, as well as the consequent decline in the incidence of formal collective contracts regulating working hours, which dropped from 62 per cent in 1992–93 to 55 per cent in 1994–95 (Crawford, Harbridge and Hince, 1996, ibid.).

In France, work on Sundays has spread since the 1993 Act on Labour, Employment and Professional Training allowed enterprises in trade and service sectors to open on Sundays, provided the Prefect of the region where the enterprise is located authorizes this, and the enterprises rely only on those employees who volunteer to work on Sundays. Subsequently, many businesses, particularly shops in tourist areas, have obtained authorization to open on Sundays. In the manufacturing sector, the new possibility for Sunday working has led to an increasing use of continuous work schedules over the whole week. In the Netherlands, since 1994, the Working Time Act allows companies to tailor working time to their own individual needs and to increase their operating time, including work at weekends, although Sunday is still not considered a normal working day under the law.

In Spain, the maximum duration of the working week continues to be 40 hours, with a maximum of nine hours per day and a minimum weekly rest of one-and-a-half days. However, as mentioned earlier, collective agreements can modify this pattern and establish a variable distribution of working hours during the year. The textile industry agreement, for example, allows individual enterprises to extend the working week to 50 hours for a period of 13 weeks.

The lengthening of shop opening hours has for some time been a significant trend in many countries. A recent example of governmental initiative in this direction is the liberalization of shop opening hours in the Netherlands in 1996, allowing shops to open between 06.00 and 22.00 from Monday to Saturday, and authorizing local governments to allow shops to open for a maximum of 12 Sundays per year. More recently, flexible opening hours have spread in the banking industry and in the public service. This trend is particularly notable in many European countries as a result of increasing competition following the deregulation of the financial sector in the EU. In France and Italy, for example, a growing number of banks have their counters open on Saturdays. In Norway, bank employees and public employees work shorter hours in summer, when their aspirations for leisure are stronger and the level of activities is lower, and longer hours in winter, when there is typically more work. In Italy, post office management and unions agreed in 1996 that some post offices should remain open on public holidays. The experiment has covered the main post offices in the 15 largest cities from 08.30 to 19.30. Remaining open on these days represents the breaking of a major "taboo" in Italian public services. During the experimental period of opening hours on public holidays, the post offices concerned were staffed by employees on three-month fixed-term contracts. In France, under a collective agreement signed in January 1997, the opening hours of many offices of the public electricity company (EDF) have been extended both on a daily (06.00 to 20.00) and a weekly (six days per week) basis. These changes have been introduced in exchange for a reduction in working hours.

Flexible working hours are also spreading in some Latin American countries, where they have traditionally been rigidly regulated by legislation. In Brazil, the so-called "rigid" Constitution of 1988 introduced a wide degree of flexibility in working time. Although it established the "traditional" working day of eight hours and a working week of 44 hours, it allowed collective agreements to change the working hours and establish the appropriate compensation for extra hours (either in payment or in days of leave). In recent years, collective agreements in large multinational companies in particular have made increasing use of this alternative, as will be explained in more detail in Chapter 5.

In Argentina, the National Employment Law of 1991 made working time more flexible by allowing reference to average working time for a week, a month, a quarter, half a year and a full year. In recent years, collective agreements have made increasing use of this alternative. One example is the collective agreement covering employees in Metrogás SA, which establishes shifts of three or four rest days for every four working days. Similarly, in Venezuela, the established limits on working hours can be modified by agreement between employers and workers. If average hours worked over a two-month period do not exceed 44 hours per week, no overtime is payable. The agreements must establish rules for compensating hours that exceed 44 hours a week, on average, over two months. In the Venezuelan context, this measure offers important administrative flexibility as no authorization is required to justify the need for flexible working weeks.

In a number of countries, however, the flexibilization of daily and weekly working hours is still subject to restrictions, and consequently its practice is somewhat limited. In the United States, for example, the majority of workers (80 per cent in 1992) still work traditional patterns of working time (a 40-hour week comprising five eight-hour days). This is largely due to the Fair Labor Standards Act of 1938, which established this pattern for all non-supervisory employees. In the public sector, two-thirds of white-collar employees also worked a 40-hour week, while most of the remaining one-third worked between 35 and 37.5 hours a week.

In many countries, working-time reduction rather than flexible working time is still the main concern of trade unions. The Republic of Korea, known until recently for its long working hours, and for using overtime routinely as a means of enhancing working-time flexibility, witnessed a drop in average monthly working hours from 237.7 in 1986 to 207 soon after the reduction of statutory working hours in 1989. More recently, with the growth of union pressure since 1996, a 40-hour, five-day working week has been introduced through collective bargaining in a number of companies. In others, alternate five-day and six-day weeks are worked, with every other Saturday off. This trend is expected to spread to small companies as workers' demands for shorter hours and more significant rest periods grow. Similarly, in Japan, the reduction of working time was one of the main labour relations issues in the early 1990s, and in European countries, more flexible working hours have often been achieved as a response to union demand for shorter working hours.

New methods of compensating overtime

The flexibilization or reduction of working hours will have little practical effect on the actual level of working hours unless overtime work is kept within reasonable limits. While some overtime is essential to give enterprises the flexibility needed to deal with unusual pressures of work resulting from fluctuating demand or other special circumstances, frequent and substantial recourse to overtime can virtually negate statutory or negotiated provisions on normal working hours, and may lead to increases in actual hours worked that are prejudicial to workers' health, safety and well-being. Where overtime is virtually institutionalized, payments represent an important, routinely expected component of earnings, and workers – especially the lowest paid –tend to count upon them as part of their remuneration. However, excessive recourse to overtime, subject to higher-rated compensation, can become a labour cost which is difficult for enterprises to bear (see Clerc, 1985, Ch. 3).

Efforts have therefore been made in many countries to minimize the cost of overtime work. An increasingly widespread measure is to grant compensatory rest time instead of extra overtime payments. In some sectors, such as hotels and restaurants, this has been a widespread practice for many years, but it has now begun spreading to other sectors in many countries. Compensatory leave is not given simply to enable workers to recuperate from excessive work, but also to enhance the operational efficiency of the enterprise. For example, if workers accumulate rest periods and go on long leave when the level of activity is low, enterprises can adapt staffing levels to fluctuating activities without incurring additional labour costs. In France, for example, an increasing number of enterprises are reported to be compensating overtime work by giving additional rest periods, rather than paying higher hourly rates. In Italy, Act No 196/1997 ("*norme in materia di promozioni della occupazione*") allowed the compensation of overtime through rest time (to be taken in periods of low activity) instead of pay. Furthermore, a recent pay accord for the railway company introduced the concept of a "working-time bank", with a 120-hour annual threshold. Under this scheme, a worker will be paid overtime rates only if the extra hours worked exceed the 120-hour threshold over a year.

The rate of overtime compensation is itself changing in many countries. In Spain, overtime used to be compensated at 175 per cent of the ordinary hourly rate, and night hours were compensated at 125 per cent. In both cases, an Act of 1994 to revise the 1980 Workers' Charter eliminated the minimum rate and left collective agreements free to determine the rates for overtime and night work. As a result, only a few companies have maintained the old standard rates, for example BP Petróleo and the brewery Cruzcampo. Others have maintained the standard 175 per cent for overtime, but compensate it with free time – a practice favoured by trade unions. Some examples can be found in GEC Alsthom, Hidroeléctrica de Cataluña, Caja Postal, Alcatel Cable Ibérica and AEG Energía. In general, however, most enterprises appear to have taken advantage of the flexibility provided by the law to conclude collective agreements with levels of compensation lower than the previous standard. In Sanyo, for example, the first ten hours of overtime are compensated at 175 per cent and the following 30 hours at 140 per cent, while the rest are compensated at the ordinary hourly rate. Ertisa, a metallurgical enterprise, compensates all additional hours at 130 per cent. Renault compensates every additional hour worked with one hour of free time, while the Ceramics and Glass sectoral agreement establishes a rate of 140 per cent, compensated in free time.

Moving away from rigid overtime regimes has been facilitated in New Zealand by the possibility, mentioned earlier, of having weekends defined as part of the working week. As many as 45 per cent of the workers covered by collective agreements in 1995–96 no longer enjoyed special rates (so-called "penal rates") for Sunday work (Harbridge and Crawford, 1997, cited in the New Zealand country study). Where these rates still apply, they seem to have been substantially reduced – for example, from double-time to time-and-a-half rates for Saturday afternoon work and triple-time payments for Sunday have been abandoned. Some contracts have moved towards a blurring of the distinction between penal and overtime rates. Furthermore, overtime is now paid for hours actually worked outside regular hours, in contrast to the past practice of paying for a predetermined period, irrespective of whether or not the workers worked during the whole period. A somewhat similar development has occurred in India, where an increasing number of collective agreements now provide that overtime will be paid only if people are physically present. This is in contrast to the so-called "guaranteed overtime" agreements that existed in a number of enterprises in India, which allowed workers to claim a predetermined amount of overtime pay irrespective of whether they were present or absent during those extra hours. The new types of collective agreements on hours of work in India seek to enhance punctuality and regularity in attendance at the workplace.

On the other hand, Fujitsu in Japan has introduced "fixed-sum" overtime pay, to be paid irrespective of whether the individual worker has worked more or less than the hours used to calculate the lump sum. In contrast with the developments in New Zealand and India, this innovation seeks to make the costs of overtime, as well as employees' earnings, more predictable than under traditional arrangements.

The search for the means of reducing overtime costs may sometimes lead to its logical (although abusive) conclusion, namely overtime without compensation. Australia, for example, has recently seen a growth in unpaid overtime work, resulting from working-time arrangements introduced by some enterprise agreements. And during the period of rapid economic development in Japan, enterprises in sectors such as banking were known to have recourse to unpaid overtime.

Clearly, traditional notions of working time, with prescribed daily and weekly working hours, have been seriously disrupted and replaced by more individualized and flexible working-time arrangements. These changes hold important implications for workers, their families and society as a whole as the demarcation line between work and leisure time continues to blur. Those implications may well differ depending upon the worker's personal profile: a single worker with no family responsibilities is more likely to be in a position to adopt a flexible schedule than a parent who needs to take into account the fixed hours of a day-care centre, school or children's bedtime – or indeed a worker with elder-care responsibilities.

Work organization flexibility

Traditional work organization, as epitomized by Frederick Taylor's theory of "scientific management", established a workplace where front-line workers had very little control over their jobs. Work was subdivided into minutely defined tasks that could be performed by semi-skilled or unskilled workers, and any decision-making power or authority was left to managers and supervisors. The image of an assembly-line worker, continuously repeating the same simple, monotonous task throughout the working day, best characterizes this style of work organization.

Technological change, customer demand for higher-quality goods and services, increasing global competition and a better-educated workforce have all contributed towards the push for greater flexibility in the way work is organized. Flexibilization of work organization has meant a move away from the rigid, Taylorist style of working towards more variable work practices, where the enterprise can more readily deploy and switch workers among different tasks as the demand for labour changes. These new forms of work organization have included such changes as dismantling job classifications, cross-training workers to perform multiple tasks and promoting teamwork.

The primary benefit cited for flexible work organization is that it can provide a key source of competitive advantage. Many employers have discovered that they can increase competitiveness by introducing changes in work organization, including streamlining work practices, reducing the number of job classifications, expanding job definitions and promoting greater cooperation and teamwork. This typically entails the participation of, and input from, workers in running the organization. Employers benefit from having front-line workers contribute their first-hand knowledge and expertise, and workers benefit from having a forum for their ideas and concerns.

According to Australian researchers, three principal factors influence the degree to which new forms of work organization are adopted. The first is the nature of the firm or industry, particularly its degree of exposure to international competition. The second is the quality of labour-management relations, especially the willingness of employers to involve employees and unions in decisions regarding changes in work organization. The third is the application of new technology and the degree of technological change influencing the need for developing new forms of work organization to be developed (Australia country study). In the Australian banking industry, for example, changes in work organization were driven by the twin objectives of cost cutting and improving customer service. Substantial changes were made to the branch structure of banking, including movement towards a "hub and spoke" design. Management and lending activities in a given geographical area were centralized, while a number of surrounding branches had their functions greatly reduced so that they performed a smaller range of less complex transitions, leading to changes in the traditional work roles of tellers and managers. Although the range of processing tasks was reduced, the depth of knowledge and skills required by branch staff to perform their new sales role increased. This was especially true of staff in regional banks, who were required to become even more multi-skilled.

Similar structural changes have recently taken place in the banking industry in France, where increasing competition has forced banks to diversify the services they offer. Rather than pursuing a traditional, "segmented" approach to banking, where different bank personnel provide distinct services to clients, tellers were expected to offer a more "integrated" service approach. A single teller could be expected to perform an array of duties such as: buying and selling shares for clients using the Minitel system; providing clients with account balances through their computers; arranging appointments with customers wishing to take out small loans and checking their credit history; and buying and selling foreign exchange directly over the counter (O'Reilly, 1994, p. 94). In addition to performing these tasks, the French tellers were also expected to do low-grade administrative work such as encoding cheques. The high degree of functional flexibility among these tellers was facilitated by their relatively high qualifications and skill levels, particularly in comparison with tellers in other countries. This was a function of the recruitment practices of French banks, which sought to raise the standard entry requirements of new employees so that they would be more adaptable to future changes.

As the above examples from the banking industry demonstrate, workers within a restructured work environment commonly need to be more knowledgeable, better educated and trained, and more adaptable than ever before. Rather than performing a single task, they are often required to perform a variety of duties, on a rotating basis, and assume increasing levels of responsibility on the job. Workplaces have also begun putting a stronger emphasis on continuous quality improvement, which demands more flexibility in work arrangements and greater reliance on workers' skills and abilities.

Some unions and employers have turned to labour-management committees as a means of reviewing, assessing, implementing, managing and evaluating various types of workplace practices. The Canadian Union of Public Employees (CUPE), for example, frequently appoints labour-management committees to study issues involving innovative work practices. In various agreements settled in 1995, CUPE called for the establishment of a telecommuting committee, a job-sharing committee and a flexible work arrangements committee, each of which were charged with studying these issues in greater depth. They were then expected to report their findings and recommendations to the bargaining committee prior to starting the contract renewal process. If representatives from labour and management agreed to the committee's recommendations, they could be implemented informally, before the next bargaining round.

Despite the growing need for greater flexibility on the job, not all attempts to introduce changes in work organization have run as smoothly as the above examples from Australia and Canada. To illustrate the complexity of movements from one mode of work organization to another, particularly in developing countries, it is useful to consider the case of the Republic of Korea. Korean firms have advanced very quickly in a relatively short period of time, but they still appear to be halfway between Taylorist forms of work organization and more innovative work practices.

Work organization in the Republic of Korea at the onset of industrialization in the 1960s was characterized by a high degree of division of labour, a low degree of worker discretion, close supervision, and minimal interaction among workers. The factory *saemel* movement, however, sought to introduce team organization aimed at reducing costs, improving quality and increasing production. An integral part of this movement was the emphasis on eliciting the "tacit" skill of employees, learned through production, in order to facilitate the introduction of imported technology and work processes. A key stumbling-block in the move towards multi-skilling and job rotation, however, has been the weak skill base among Korean workers. The lack of a highly trained and skilled workforce has led to problems of quality and cost, which have given rise to experiments with quality circles.

The different perspectives of workers and management have also forestalled the smooth transition to more flexible work organization. For example, Korean workers seemed more intent on introducing job rotation out of a desire to equalize or share job intensity, rather than as a means of promoting multi-skilling. This is corroborated by the fact that union members and their representatives at the shop-floor level, having succeeded in reducing the power of supervisors and foremen in controlling labour, have become more interested in working conditions and work assignment issues. But they remain negative or at best passive regarding productivity and quality issues, viewing these as typically employers' concerns. Similarly, they have not voiced a clear position on training and skills development, while employers have shown a desire to introduce further automation, as a means of circumventing what they see as conflictual attitudes on the part of the workforce.

The successful introduction of work organization flexibility depends on a number of factors, not least a commitment from both management and workers to implement these changes. As compared to the other forms of flexibility discussed earlier, changes in work organization require more active involvement and participation of workers. For instance, in a restructured work environment, workers are typically called upon to use their problem-solving capacities, rather than relying on management to resolve every issue that arises.

Of equal importance is the extent to which work practice reform goes hand in hand with other types of flexibility, namely changes in wages, employment contracts and working time. For example, combining a variety of sophisticated work practices to achieve work organization flexibility with a programme of mass lay-offs is unlikely to achieve the desired functional flexibility sought in lean production. Thus, the question of "procedural flexibility" – or procedural soundness and accept-ability, and how it is used to achieve the right mix of flexibilities – becomes a key consideration. The next section considers different experiments with achieving work organization flexibility, especially means of overcoming occupational demarcations, and experiments in teamwork and direct participation by workers.

Overcoming occupational demarcations through skill enhancement

Efforts to move away from work organization based on rigid occupational demarcations are not totally new phenomena. In addition to the Fawley produc-tivity agreements of 1960 referred to earlier, several other initiatives aimed at flexibilizing work organization had gained popularity throughout the industrialized world by the first half of the 1970s. These were often referred to as "quality of working life" (QWL) movements or "humanization of work" programmes, reflecting the growing recognition of the negative effects of rigid occupational demarcations on both productivity and workers' job satisfaction.

The changes currently taking place, however, are different from the earlier changes in their objectives and effects. While the work reforms of the 1970s sought to enhance productivity through improving working conditions and reducing the economic costs of various manifestations of workers' discontent with the prevailing forms of work organization, the current drives for work reform seek above all to optimize the use of human capabilities in a particular production system. They are also affecting working conditions in many workplaces more significantly than previous attempts, as opposition to the changes is weaker because of the stronger bargaining power of employers and a wider consensus on the need for work reforms.

Countries with a tradition of rigid occupational demarcations, such as the United Kingdom, Australia, New Zealand, Canada and the United States, have generally faced the strongest pressures for reforming work organization, as well as the greatest challenges in doing so. In the Scandinavian countries, for example, work reforms have been a relatively gradual process of change since the 1970s; in other countries, such as Japan, occupational demarcations have traditionally been flexible.

Approaches to reducing occupational demarcations vary widely. In the United Kingdom, for example, job evaluation has been an important tool in moving away from occupational demarcations of traditional grade and wage classifications. There have also been efforts to harmonize systems of classifying white-collar and blue-collar workers, in order to bring these categories into the same classification structure. However, these efforts have met with only mitigated success.

New Zealand presents a dramatic example of the move away from occupational demarcation. Prior to 1991, it had a national occupational structure, with very strict demarcation lines and other work rules in most industries, particularly in large enterprises. The fact that different workers could be operating side by side, under different agreements, with different terms and conditions of employment, created a severe impediment to functional flexibility, especially because technological changes have tended to blur the traditional distinctions between the work of one craft and another. Then, as part of the sweeping changes to the labour laws enacted in 1991, New Zealand moved away from national occupational awards towards broader occupational classifications. Rapid changes in functional flexibility ensued. According to a 1992 study based upon a sample of 1,335 enterprises, 55 per cent of employers reported five or fewer occupational classifications. In addition, 70 per cent reported employing different grades and categories of staff in each classification, a clear sign of functional flexibility (Ryan, 1992, cited in the New Zealand country study). A 1996 study found that 38 per cent of managers stated that the level of demarcations had been reduced, and 48 per cent reported an increase in multi-skilling (NZIER, 1996).

Australia, at least until 1996, tried a more centralized approach to overcoming occupational demarcations and promoting skill acquisition. In the metal industry, under the influence of the "restructuring and efficiency" principle elaborated by the Australian Industrial Relations Commission (AIRC) in 1987, the old award system was reorganized into a new classification structure establishing professional career progression based on the level of work complexity, as well as the completion of training modules. In essence, it provided a means of evaluating the skill of the individual worker independently of the particular post or job, with the skill endorsed by a national training board. Workers were also rendered more employable in the process, as they were eligible to work across enterprises within the sector. The metal industry classification served as a model for other sectors in Australia, such as motor manufacturing, construction, textiles and journalism.

In Norway, the focus on multi-skilling has been advanced by the Government's objective of facilitating workforce mobility throughout the national labour market. Firms have focused on the idea of reducing the high degree of workforce specialization, and have concluded collective agreements designed to enable individual workers to perform a wide range of tasks. In line with national policy to promote a more flexible labour force, with multiple skills and updated qualifications, adult training and permanent education have been developed throughout the country, and a reform of the apprenticeship system has been conducted.

The motor industry in France has also been moving towards the development of a multi-skilled workforce. The industry today tends to comprise only assembly plants and research departments, while entire sections of activity have been outsourced. This major industry restructuring has resulted in new forms of work organization. In order to improve economic performance and to increase its market share, the French car manufacturer Renault, for example, has introduced a number of initiatives to accompany an important change in the production system. These include the following:

- the occupational hierarchy has been reduced;
- in several departments, work has been organized in small basic units, each in charge of a homogeneous production task (integrated assembly line, project group, etc);
- within basic units, workers are multi-skilled, which was supported by a training programme over several years.

In cases where more centralized attention to skill training to achieve functional flexibility has not been forthcoming, trade unions have sometimes taken a lead, conscious of the need to enhance their members' capacity to meet the challenges of economic pressures in their industry. The Communications, Energy and Paperworkers' Union in Canada, which represents workers in the forestry and mill industries, recently negotiated a series of collective agreements focusing on "trades flexibility". The goal was to reduce barriers between workers in various skilled trades and promote collaborative work on projects, rather than having workers wait to carry out that part of the job directly related to their trade. This was in the interest of creating a multi-skilled, cross-trained workforce, able to minimize downtime and thereby improve efficiency and productivity. This example is illustrative of a broader trend towards skills upgrading through negotiations: in 1994, only 19 per cent of collective agreements in Canada had provisions for training, while in 1995, the proportion had jumped to 49 per cent.

The issue of skill development for functional flexibility is much more complicated in developing and newly industrializing countries, where educational systems are frequently weak and usually not sufficiently geared towards industry and its rapidly evolving requirements. Where national training and skills certification boards do exist, they are often not sufficiently valued by industry as they tend to be out of touch with industrial reality. There have been some notable attempts to rectify the situation, however. For example, the National Skills Development Funds in Malaysia and Singapore, established on a tripartite basis with joint funding from government and management, have been a source of considerable industry-specific training in those countries – as well as an inspiration for other industrializing countries.

Influenced by these countries' efforts, India's Standing Labour Committee of the Tripartite Labour Conference has initiated discussions on establishing a similar body to upgrade the skill profile of the workforce and prepare for upcoming changes in industrial employment as the economy continues to open and expand. The idea is to finance the Fund from a 2 per cent levy on enterprises' annual turnover. The establishment of a statutory trade testing and certification board is also under serious consideration. In the meantime, the existing Central Apprenticeship Council has recommended that a number of new, multi-skilled trades be designated, such as operator – industrial automation, industrial electronics mechanic, and plant mechanic – transmission and distribution. Although these developments may not seem revolutionary, they represent important steps towards changing the typically fixed, rigid occupational classifications that have characterized much of industry in developing countries.

To make up for the lack of a national-level focus on skill enhancement in newly industrializing and developing countries, some individual enterprises have begun focusing on overcoming occupational demarcations. Such is the case in the motor industry in Brazil, where multi-skilling has been addressed in a few recent agreements. Under the Mercedes Benz agreement of 1993, for example, the number of occupations was reduced from 419 to 250. The remaining jobs are classified into four different functions: A for support; B for semi-skilled; C for skilled; and D for specialized workers. Similarly, the 1996 agreement signed at Black & Decker with the Uberaba Metal Union also incorporates the idea of multi-skilled workers.

Multi-skilling is a recurrent issue in most recent agreements in Argentina, although there is considerable variation among the various agreements in how this is regulated. The plastics industry agreement, for instance, establishes 14 different job categories and, although it adopts the principle of task stability, it introduces the possibility of establishing other forms of work or categories not contemplated in the agreement if the employer and the union agree. A similar approach has been adopted by the food industry agreement, which describes the existing categories in detail (more than 40 pages), but also establishes the multi-skilling principle in the interests of productive efficiency. Many agreements make a detailed list of categories, leaving open the possibility of assigning workers to other functions in response to service needs. This has been the case, for example, at Obras Sanitarias (water), Metrogas (gas) and Edenor (electricity).

Some agreements in Argentina adopt a broad approach to multi-skilling, listing just a few categories with very broad job descriptions. The most extreme case is the contract between Toyota and the Union of Engineering and Related Workers in Motor Transport (SMATA), which establishes only two categories of workers: "multi-skilled worker" and "multi-skilled worker-group leader". Following this trend, the agreements signed by General Motors and Chrysler with the same union include just four job functions, while the Fiat agreement establishes six categories.

Teamwork

The dismantling of occupational demarcations has coincided with the spread of teamwork, as workers are cross-trained to perform multiple tasks, rather than focusing on individual work assignments. Teamwork has also called into question the traditional demarcation lines between labour and management, as workers often have greater opportunity to influence the content of their jobs and make decisions previously left to managerial prerogative.

The Swedish motor industry provides a prime example of the move to highly autonomous work teams. In 1991 Volvo's Torslanda plant launched a programme of "Quality, Precise delivery and Economy" (QPE) to improve product delivery and speed up the process of model renewal. Teamwork became an essential part of the programme objective, with teams introduced in the assembly sector, the paint shop and the body shop. The teams are self-regulated, participate in change and development, and carry out their own follow-up of the production outcome. In addition to their pure production work, they carry out maintenance, troubleshoot problems, plan future activities and keep in touch with subcontractors. The idea is to make the QPE teams skilled both as customers and suppliers in the company's internal relations.

The new teamwork organization at Torslanda excludes traditional supervisors, as they are replaced with "production leaders". These are team members with overall responsibility for the manufacturing process, who also handle financial issues. The position of team leader is held on a rotating basis among the whole team. To ensure that the team members are performing different tasks (multi-skilling), the work assignments also rotate among members.

This type of teamwork is characterized by a high degree of group autonomy in terms of selecting team members and leaders, and in assigning work within the team. It is also characterized by an absence of hierarchy and a high degree of multi-skilling aimed at making each member capable of carrying out several functions. In practice, there are few examples of such teams, either in Scandinavia or in other countries. In Germany, for example, only 0.6 per cent of mechanical engineering companies were reportedly using work teams in which there was no hierarchy among members, and members carried out some planning and non-manufacturing activities and had homogeneous and multiple skills, with job rotation (Sauerwein, cited in Ozaki, 1996b).

Another form of teamwork has originated in Japan, where workers' assignments within a work unit are not rigidly divided along functional lines, and each member of a work unit is trained to carry out several tasks assigned to the unit, rather than focusing on a single task. Yet all team members do not carry out all tasks. Unlike the Scandinavian teamwork model, the supervisors or group leaders in Japanese organizations continue to play a key hierarchical role. These leaders are nominated by management, and have a major say in designing individual tasks and training workers. The teams comprise members with different levels of seniority and skill, integrated into the hierarchical lines of authority of the enterprise. As they acquire seniority and new skills, team members are expected to move upwards in the group. Several carefully defined basic tasks with different degrees of difficulty are grouped to make up each worker's job. The same tasks are purposely assigned to several workers – who have different levels of experience – in order to encourage mutual support and on-the-job training (OJT). The team leaders and senior members of the group are expected to be able to carry out all the group tasks, and to guide and advise less experienced group members. Thus teamwork provides a highly effective framework for OJT in Japan.

Since the concept of teamwork differs from country to country, and often from one enterprise to another within the same country, it is difficult to characterize the proliferation of teamwork *per se.*

In the Japanese motor industry, for example, virtually all production workers – about two-thirds of the workforce – are reportedly working in groups. However, a 1993 survey showed that 40 per cent of enterprises were placing a growing emphasis on individual work assignments, while only 25 per cent were moving towards the further strengthening of their group-based work organization.

Other countries, however, are exhibiting a fairly rapid growth in group-based work. In the United States, for example, a 1990 survey of the 1,000 companies graded by Fortune magazine showed that 47 per cent had work teams, a jump from just 28 per cent in 1987. However, such findings need to be tempered by more detailed information on the actual scope of these schemes. Thus, only 10 per cent were applying teamwork to over 20 per cent of employees (as compared to 7 per cent in 1987); and in only 1 per cent of the companies were more than 40 per cent of employees involved in teamwork. A different survey carried out by the National Center on Education and the Economy in 1994 revealed that 12 per cent of non-managerial workers participated in self-managed teams, and 17 per cent in job rotation.

In the German mechanical engineering industry, 29 per cent of companies reported the incidence of group work in 1991. But the increase in teamwork has been most dramatic in the German motor industry, as the percentage of production workers operating in groups rose from 9 per cent in 1993 to 22 per cent one year later. This sharp increase is largely due to a decision by Audi in 1994 to introduce teamwork.

In Australia, a 1991 survey of 2,000 workplaces employing more than 20 workers found that one-third had introduced significant changes in work practices or technology, with only 14 per cent saying they had introduced no change at all. Interestingly, the public sector was nearly twice as likely to have restructured work practices as the private sector – 49 per cent as compared to 28 per cent. The survey also investigated the presence of job design, semi-autonomous work groups, and quality circles or team building. Of the workplaces reporting significant changes in work practices, nearly half used none of these practices, while 31 per cent used only one practice, 15 per cent used two and just 6 per cent employed all three practices. Using another indicator to measure the extent of technical and/or organizational flexibility (including just-in-time (JIT) production, total quality control and computer-integrated management), 25 per cent of the companies demonstrated a high level of flexibility and 70 per cent a low level. This would appear to reflect the fact that few firms have been able to introduce both qualitative and quantitative changes in the area of functional flexibility.

Although the available data do not present a clear picture of the changes under way in work organization, it appears that practices such as multi-skilling and teamwork are not yet widespread. There are numerous reasons for this. One is that unions, for the most part, have been reluctant to adopt such schemes, largely due to the threat they pose to trade union autonomy. There are exceptions, however, where unions themselves have played a leading role in introducing work reforms. (This issue will be discussed further in Chapter 4.) Another reason is that a major change in work organization requires a strong commitment from top management and the involvement of all employees. It is only in this way that leaders can draw upon the knowledge that the workforce has developed by being close to the product and the client. Few organizations, however, have been able to successfully make the break from traditional, hierarchical work systems to ones in which front-line workers play a more active role.

Nevertheless, many high-performing enterprises have emerged which exhibit some of the characteristics discussed above. Partly as a result, there is an increasing diffusion of such practices. Thus, while few organizations have been able to make the break from hierarchical work systems, the trend is still heading in that direction. Changes in the views of effective management would probably accelerate this trend.

MEANS OF INTRODUCING FLEXIBILITY

2

Introduction

Flexibility measures may be introduced by means of legislation, collective bargaining, individual employment contracts, unilateral action by employers or a combination of these methods. But what is the best mix? This chapter explores the respective roles of each of these means and examines the linkages among them in various countries. It also points towards a synergistic model involving legislation, collective bargaining and other means that could optimize the introduction of flexibility within a framework of a well-functioning system of collective labour relations and individual employment relationships.

Flexibility is inherently relative. A discussion of the relationship of flexibility to legislation, collective bargaining, individual employment contracts and unilateral employers' action cannot begin without recognizing that each system has a different starting-point. The legal and labour relations systems of the world display considerable diversity. Yet it is possible to identify two principal approaches to labour relations (coordinated and individualized or "voluntarist") and two major legal systems (civil law and common law, although there are many hybrids that also add features of their own). These differences influence the approach taken to introducing flexibility in various contexts, as do ideological policy orientations. Yet employers everywhere can take an array of decisions to promote greater flexibility at work, given the power they enjoy in their relationship with workers. However, *which* decisions employers may take with a basically free hand does vary by country, and the leeway will obviously be less where legislative or collectively bargained provisions extensively govern the field.

The respective roles of legislation, collective bargaining, individual employment contracts and unilateral managerial action may also differ depending on the aspect of flexibility at stake (numerical, functional or financial) and the subject-matter being addressed. Moreover, the roles may diverge depending on the category of workers concerned, since the coverage of various types of legislation and of collective agreements may well differ for various industries, for employees in the private and public sectors, and for special categories of workers.

To risk a generalization, it may be said that the respective roles of legislation, collective bargaining, individual employment contracts and employers' unilateral action in relation to flexibility measures are determined by three main factors:

* legal rules governing the framework for collective labour relations and individual terms and conditions of employment;
* the extent to which collective bargaining is actually used in practice; and
* the way in which employers exercise their managerial prerogatives.

Once these are identified, it is possible to perceive the space that is left for individual agreement between the employer and the worker. All the means reflect the relative positions of labour and capital, and here a paradox emerges: legislation, collective bargaining and the parameters for contracts of employment are based at the national level or below, whereas employers' strategy for action is increasingly transnational. Yet employers and their suppliers still operate within the boundaries of national legislation and any collective agreements that may be applicable to the workers concerned. The limitations on that legislation are seen not only in the changing role of the State, but also in the increasing difficulty that labour law has in coming to grips with new forms of production and work organization. As Hyman has observed, the role of the State in labour markets appears to be shifting "from mediating the conflicting interests of capital and labour to acquiescing in the demands of employers for increased autonomy" (Hyman, 1998, p. 188).

A somewhat artificial typology of three approaches to flexibility can be perceived: flexibility driven by legislation (as in Australia, France, Spain, and New Zealand in 1991); flexibility driven by collective bargaining (as in Denmark, Ireland, Italy, the Netherlands and Norway); and flexibility driven by individual employers' initiatives (as in multinational enterprises operating in union-free environments, India, New Zealand today, Peru, non-union enterprises in the United States, etc.). Any or all of these may be reflected in individual relationships, especially contracts of employment. Yet this typology is artificial, since whether a country may be categorized as having flexibility driven mainly by legislation or by collective bargaining, there is an obvious synergy between the two processes. Legislation is often arrived at after a consensus has been hammered out through bargaining, and collective bargaining innovations often need the impetus of legislative changes, upon which they may build. The balance may also differ depending upon the subject-matter at issue.

When examining, in any particular system, the relationship of legislation, collective bargaining, individual employment contracts and employers' unilateral decisions as regards flexibility measures, several initial questions must be posed: What is the hierarchy of norms in the legal system? Do collective agreements have binding force in law? And may collective agreements diverge from national law, and if so, to what extent? And individual agreements from law and/or from collective agreements? What percentage and which categories of employees are covered by collective agreements? And by individual contracts of employment? Do works' councils play an important role in the country? If so, what is their relationship to collective bargaining? What are the trends? Do they differ by industry? Are employers' decisions motivated by a transnational strategy or by a more ad hoc domestic approach? The replies may have a significant impact on the interplay of the various elements affecting the introduction of flexibility measures in practice, and may point to factors which influence the choice of collective bargaining as a means of doing this.

Legislation

Nature and function

Legislation is a basic instrument for regulating collective labour relations and individual employment relationships. It is the product of compromise between competing political forces representing more than workers' and employers' interests. Its content may reflect not only a compromise on the subject-matter of a particular statute, but also broader political trade-offs between that subject and others competing for the lawmakers' attention. In countries in which complex parliamentary procedures defy swift action, legislation is a technique that resists rapid change. Added to this is the unpredictable nature of the political process that produces legislation, in which pressure groups of various types can exert influence well beyond their numerical importance.

Legislation inevitably sets common rules to address what may be a wide variety of circumstances, although exclusions and exceptions are of course part and parcel of legislative drafting. While it may be necessary to amend statutes and regulations that stand in the way of certain types of desired flexibility, legislation is by nature a less satisfactory method for promoting flexibility than a process that is controlled primarily by the parties to the labour relationship. On the other hand, legislation may reflect broader interests and values than the parties directly involved and may permit the expression of wider societal concerns, such as a perceived need to combat social exclusion, preserve some hours in a week for religious, social and/or family life, or promote greater labour force participation by women.[1] Sometimes legislation is the direct outcome of collective bargaining, as in Ireland, where negotiations lead to employment regulation orders, which set legally binding pay and conditions for all employers in the sectors covered – although these comprise only about 8 to 9 per cent of employees in the country (Ireland country study).

It is also indispensable for setting out the minimum "rules of the game" in the labour field and, for the many millions of workers worldwide not covered by collective agreements, employment legislation affords virtually the only means of protection. Moreover, legislation can bring to bear the entire means of action of the State. For instance, in an attempt to promote employment, the State may invent a new legal category of contract, such as training contracts, and at the same time offer fiscal incentives to firms that use them. State power can also back up the implementation of legislation with the full panoply of institutions that have been created to enforce its laws (although they may be too weak to do so convincingly in certain cases). And when legislation takes a radically new approach, as seen in Australia recently and in New Zealand and Peru earlier, the effects on labour relations can be far-reaching and profound.

Furthermore, cultural attitudes towards legislation and towards law in general differ somewhat from country to country. In civil law systems, administrative action is seen as being based on the innate powers of the State, whereas judicial action needs a grounding in legislation. Civil law reasoning has been characterized as "institutional", being more concerned with principles than facts. Common law proceeds from the power of the judiciary to hand down the law as adduced from a set of facts, and its approach is essentially empirical. These differing approaches can matter when it comes to collective and individual relationships between labour and capital.

In addition, while in theory everyone would agree that legislation of its nature should be respected, there is in fact a range of tolerance of non-compliance that differs widely from country to country. Although difficult to measure, this factor is important in assessing the relative impact that legislation will actually have in a given situation. (To some extent this may be a reflection of the size of the informal sector, where operating outside the law may in part define such activities (ILO, 1997, pp. 185 and 187).) Legal restrictions are sometimes more apparent

---

[1] Encouraging the employment of women can be done quite indirectly, such as through the approach taken by a country's social security system. In a comparison of policy on working time and atypical employment, it was found that Sweden's approach to social security protection (with each individual having entitlements), compared with that of Austria (assuming that there was a dependent spouse in a couple, usually the woman), had important effects both on recourse to part-time work and on women's labour force participation rates. These legal arrangements created structural constraints that could not be overcome by collective bargaining (S. Widmar: Arbeitspolitik und atypische Arbeitszeitgestaltung, May 1997, unpublished).

than real.[2] People may do what they can to get around the law by inventing new types of work relationship. Similarly, the parties' knowledge of the law and their ability to use it will influence its effect in practice.

As long as the performance of work involves dependence on capital, labour law will continue to be part of any legal order that claims to guarantee respect for the individual (Simitis, 1997, p. 667). Yet the coexistence of individual and collective rights gives labour legislation its peculiar flavour. This has led to a recent description of the function of labour law in terms of four approaches:

The first regards collective bargaining as the primary source of protection for workers, but is prepared to allow legal intervention to protect workers who fall outside of the collective bargaining sphere. The second aims to underpin collective bargaining with individual rights, extending to workers both within and outside the collective bargaining arena ... . The third legal response is diametrically different. Far from using labour law to create an equilibrium, it aims to "reduce the burdens on business", and thereby facilitate a low-cost flexible workforce ... . The fourth approach, still in its infancy, is one which seeks to refashion labour law to accommodate both the move to flexibility and the needs and rights of workers [including, importantly, non-standard workers].[3]

The law in many countries establishes the legal framework for labour relations, sometimes covering not only collective bargaining but other forms of worker representation as well, such as works councils. In a country where work councils are well developed, such as Germany, they are the vehicle for introducing certain innovations relating to work organization. In Germany, works councils and collective bargaining complement one another, and the legislation establishing works councils sets out an implicit framework for that purpose.

Labour legislation reflects "normal" work relationships and values about them at a particular historical time (see Däubler, 1988, cited in Vidmar, 1997, pp. 44–45). The "normal" definition of labour law serves three functions: protection (minimum legal standards to protect workers, given their unequal bargaining power, from dumping in the labour market; this also embraces a "moral" function of avoiding unacceptable levels of exploitation); promotion (to force social acceptance of an idea within the market economy); and a selection/ distribution function to divide up the volume of work in the labour market among a maximum number of workers while also keeping some out of the labour market, such as those who cannot offer full-time workforce participation (Mückenberger, 1989, cited in Vidmar, 1997, p. 45; Däubler, 1998, ibid.). Yet it is precisely the definition of "normal" that is

---

[2] This experience is clearly shown in India (India country study), but is by no means reserved to developing countries. The same phenomenon was seen in Italy with regard to unrealistic restrictions that applied previously to recruitment for employment — they were simply ignored (Italy country study).

[3] S. Fredman: "Labour law in flux: The changing composition of the workforce," in *Industrial Law Journal* (London), Vol. 26, No. 4, Dec. 1997, pp. 340-341. See also H. Collins, "The productive disintegration of labour law," ibid., pp. 295-309.

undergoing profound change, and this in turn calls for new approaches in labour legislation which are only beginning to emerge. Labour legislation represents regulatory intervention in the labour market, a search for equilibrium between unequal forces. Just as industrialization marked the appearance and consolidation of labour law, the new organization of work will determine its future (Simitis, 1997, p. 656). The same may be said of collective bargaining.

How rules fit together: The hierarchy of legal norms

The hierarchy of legal norms in a given system is crucial for understanding how the various rules fit together. Purely legal sources normally start with the national Constitution, followed by laws enacted by the supreme legislative authority and then by regulations or orders issued by government administrators. The Constitution itself can legitimize the possibility of using collective bargaining as a means of introducing flexible exceptions, as in Brazil and South Africa, for example. Pre-emptive norms, such as those prohibiting slavery, and general principles of law, such as the notion of public order and the rule of applying the most favourable treatment in law, also guide interpretation of how the various legal sources intermesh. Legal rules will furthermore determine whether or not workers and employers may waive their legal rights or derogate from the provisions of law. Provisions that would be incompatible with the Constitution of a country, or with fundamental rights/pre-emptory norms/precepts of public order, are not permissible. Added to this are notions of "acquired rights" in some systems, as in Latin America, with rights being cumulative and, once in place, extremely difficult to dislodge (Bronstein, 1997, p. 9).

The law will also normally determine the legal effect to be given to a collective agreement. This effect varies by country. In many civil law countries, collective agreements occupy a ranking that is below that of legal norms, but when they provide more favourable conditions than legislation, they in fact ensure a higher level of protection. Spain illustrates this point. The Workers' Charter in Spain specifies that workers cannot waive their rights, which are thus transformed into directly applicable pre-emptive legal rules to which collective agreements and individual contracts of employment must conform. Collective agreements as legal norms in Spain have the following effects: their rules automatically apply to individual relationships, thus precluding contracts between an employer and an employee that contradict or waive rights in the collective agreement; a subsequent agreement overrides an earlier one unless otherwise specified; agreements must be published officially; one party can sue another for non-compliance (in addition to administrative procedures available to the labour inspectorate); and decisions that contravene collective agreements can be legally challenged (Spain country study).

These results are not unique to civil law systems, however. India and Namibia also illustrate the common approach that collective agreements providing conditions inferior to or different from those prescribed in legislation cannot be legally enforced (India country study; Namibia Labour Act 1992).

Yet the legal system has the power to alter its own rules governing hierarchy, as long as it does not contravene the national Constitution (see, for example, Robineau, 1997, pp. 4–5). This has been done, for instance, by means of permitting collective agreements effectively to opt out of the application of legislative provisions in Austria, Italy and Spain.[4] Interpretation of laws is another source of potential flexibility or lack of it. Interpretation may come by way of regulations or administrative guidelines adopted under statutes; a good example is provided by the Explanatory Bulletins issued by the Department of Labor and Employment of the Philippines (the Philippines country study) on new trends in working time in relation to the provisions of the Labour Code. Interpretation may naturally also be made by court decisions, which in the common law system act as precedent. Even in a civil law system, the tribunals provide guidance to the parties as to what is acceptable in terms of flexible practices.[5] Overall, the courts tend to have a moderating influence; this is seen in New Zealand, for instance, where tribunals use general principles of equity and fairness in interpreting the Employment Contracts Act 1991. This has left a number of areas of the employment relationship uncharted by statute.

At the same time, the courts have sometimes taken new approaches that permit greater flexibility. German law, for instance, formerly prevented the parties from renouncing rights established under an existing agreement (Simitis, 1997, p. 660). This is now possible when there is a justification for balancing the acquired rights of workers and the reasons for rolling them back. In addition, recent French jurisprudence has authorized the substitution of rules in collective agreements for unilateral rules, even though the agreements may be less favourable

---

[4] In Spain, a new section of the Workers' Charter allows the modification of conditions set by collective agreement as to schedules, shift work, and so on, when agreed by the employer and workers' representatives; a similar type of opting out is possible for wages (Spain country study). No deviation is possible through collective bargaining in Italy if the provisions are of a "public order" nature, but the number of norms which may be changed has increased greatly in the last ten to 15 years (Italy country study). In Italy, the courts and the legislature have granted greater freedom for collective bargaining, and for workers and employers to conclude individual contracts without repealing fundamental pieces of legislation protecting workers. In Austria too, legislation sets down minimum standards, but leaves multifaceted opportunities for manoeuvre in relation to collective legal norms (Vidmar, 1997, p. 9). The law on working time permits lower-level regulation that may provide for more favourable treatment (ibid., p. 12), and this opening has been amply used in relation to collective bargaining on working time.(ibid., pp. 41 and 129–30). These alternative agreements have status as sources of law in Austria.

[5] Recent rulings of the highest courts in Italy have held that an employee may agree to be downgraded (a practice normally disallowed by the legislation of that country) when and if the arrangement proves to be more favourable, i.e. it is the only way to keep a job (Italy country study). Courts in the Philippines have taken a similar approach in approving a waiver of legally mandated overtime pay, by looking at compensatory privileges and health and safety protections enjoyed by the workers.

(Robineau, 1997, p. 3). In Brazil, the labour courts have taken positions that considerably extend the flexibility afforded on the face of the legislation. Such interpretations by the courts are sometimes condemned, but they are part of the contemporary industrial relations landscape.

Prescriptive or framework legislation

Speaking of legislation as a "source" of flexibility measures may appear misleading: the raison d'être of law is to fix rules, and rules automatically conjure up an image of rigidity. Yet these rules can differ in nature, setting absolutes or establishing frameworks. Legislation can take a prescriptive or a functional tack, depending on the legal tradition and the subject-matter being addressed. Basic guarantees such as protection against forced labour call for watertight legal statements; flexibility is not on the agenda when it comes to fundamental workers' rights. But an issue such as working hours leaves considerable room for a wide range of legislative approaches, although here too there is a need for a "floor" of minimum protection, given the physical limits of human beings and society's values about work and time outside work that are at stake. Framework legislation can fix parameters of permissible action and can set out institutional arrangements for decision-making, such as through collective bargaining.

In a country with a tradition of detailed regulation in absolute terms, legislative reform will obviously be necessary for introducing greater flexibility at work (as in France, Peru and Spain). Other countries, having adopted legislation that simply sets out a framework for relationships in the labour field, find that the law already provides a sound basis for the parties to seek greater flexibility when they so desire (for example, Ireland, Norway, Sweden). In common-law countries, where legislative enactments have essentially encroached upon what had been seen as inherent freedoms or powers (for instance, the freedom to contract and the power to hire and fire), it has been more a question of finding the appropriate level and means of protection to be introduced (particularly in relation to non-discrimination, termination of employment and working hours). Even with the legislation enacted over the past 20 years or so in the United Kingdom under the impetus of EU directives, "there is relatively little direct legal regulation of employment relations in Britain" (United Kingdom country study); the same may be said of Ireland and New Zealand. The common-law system represents "a maximum level of legal flexibility" (Ireland country study). Many areas remain in which the law does not define rights and responsibilities in relation to employment in these countries.

Brazil offers a clear example of how legislation has been used, and indeed very early on (in 1966), as the motor behind deregulation in relation to termination of employment (Brazil country study). In 1988, the new Constitution tempered this somewhat by introducing greater protection against dismissal, but basically the situation remains one of high labour mobility (average job tenure is two years). In India, by contrast, the legislation remains a source of labour market rigidity; 1977 amendments to the Industrial Disputes Act 1947 made it more difficult to lay off workers and close down the enterprise. This legislation has been heavily criticized as a constraint on introducing changes in conditions of service and as engendering reluctance among employers officially to take on new staff (India country study). Although the prospect of labour law reform at the national level remains politically elusive, some states in India have introduced legislation that aims at flexibility.

In general, the role legislation plays in the move towards flexibility very much depends upon the extent to which it is seen as a genuine source of rigidity in the first place. Where it is perceived as being highly prescriptive, it has been concluded that revision is needed. But that revision can take radically different courses, with understandably varying results. Comparisons between the approaches taken by New Zealand, Peru and the United Kingdom, for instance, and those followed by the Netherlands, Spain and Sweden, suffice to illustrate this.

The ideological belief in the effectiveness of free markets led the previous British Government to pursue a legislative strategy based on numerical flexibility, a low level of established rights and avoidance of minimum standards. The legal environment encouraged management to take initiatives in this direction. Accompanying this was a hostility to collective institutions, on both the workers' and the employers' sides, that was expressed in a series of legislative reforms. Aside from a commitment to seek legislation on trade union recognition and compensation in case of collective unfair dismissals, the Labour Government has not envisaged a major change in its approach to labour market regulation or the law; indeed, it hopes to extend flexible labour markets to the rest of Europe. Flexibility has become more or less a starting-point in the United Kingdom, and legislative change ensured that it would occur (United Kingdom country study).

Similar ideological motivation lay at the heart of legislative reforms undertaken in New Zealand, where there was an increasing perception that the industrial awards system was acting as a drag on the economy. In the industrial relations context, enactment of the Employment Contracts Act in 1991 marked a sharp break with the past. The Act both symbolized and enacted an ideological change in industrial relations. With very little guidance, it encouraged employers and employees to make their own employment contractual arrangements, with everything permissively negotiable and nothing mandatorily negotiable (McAndrew, 1992, cited in the New Zealand country study). Although under the new system some employers still see merit in collectively bargained arrangements, the coverage of such agreements is now around a quarter of the workforce and bargaining has largely been decentralized. It is in the reliance on individual contracts of employment, however, that the Act's truly radical colours are revealed, since it is based on the assumption that a contract of employment is just like a commercial contract.

The weakness of social dialogue in Peru, due in large part to the oligarchic nature of the State over many decades, has meant that it has not contributed meaningfully to flexibility issues. The failure of social dialogue over difficult economic and employment problems has forced the debate back into the legislative forum. Peru has moved from an excessively regulated labour market to one which has gone too far in removing protection for workers. This has primarily been done by creating new types of contracts other than "standard" contracts of employment, with the result that almost half the workforce no longer falls within the ambit of labour legislation. Eliminating the heavily prescriptive prior administrative authorization for dismissals was certainly reasonable, but the changes in legislation seem only to have deprived workers of their rights, rather than opening up collective bargaining as a means of filling the void. Moreover, the State remains quite interventionist in relation to collective labour relations and national minimum wages, while claiming to leave these matters to market forces. With the severe erosion of collective bargaining in Peru and indeed in the subregion, this approach leaves individual workers largely on their own, in a context of high unemployment (Peru country study).

Although collective bargaining has never been used extensively in Peru, it certainly was and is used in New Zealand and the United Kingdom. It is a testimony to the inherent usefulness and resilience of the institution that it remains a force for a significant, although certainly reduced, proportion of the working population in spite of the legal onslaught that it has suffered in those two countries. By comparison, it is interesting to note how legislation has been supportive of collective bargaining in relation to flexibility in other countries: the Netherlands, South Africa, Spain and Sweden. A closer look at Spain illustrates this.

Traditionally, Spanish legislation also heavily regulated the labour market, and for some years the social partners were at loggerheads about changing the situation. The issues were particularly sensitive because of the historical role of labour legislation in the country's return to democracy in 1975. Finally, in April 1997, a tripartite agreement was concluded, embodying a new consensus that various forms of flexibility should be introduced so as to meet the needs of both employers and workers; the parties also agreed to adaptations in various aspects of the employment relationship, and that collective bargaining should be developed and enriched as a regulating device for working conditions. Among the conclusions reached was the setting up of a Follow-up Commission to trace the effects of the reforms over a four-year period, and the adoption by government of tax measures to favour the creation of permanent jobs. The Economic and Social Council gave its endorsement to the accords, which were formally approved in a royal legislative decree in August 1997 (Spain country study). The legislation was thus changed, but in ways that took collective bargaining into account and in fact promoted its use.

Cutting across countries, the question of working time has been a major engine of legislative change. Legal flexibility in relation to working time is well exemplified by Swedish legislation.[6] Some countries set legal limits on overtime but allow them to be exceeded under a legally binding collective agreement, which has to meet certain criteria (as in Belgium). Similarly, in France, the Robien Law 1996 provides that pay determination following the reorganization of working time is a matter for collective negotiation. Elsewhere, as in Germany (see Veneziani, 1992, pp. 48–49), plant-level agreements can fix maximum hours, up to defined limits and with the possibility of averaging over certain periods. In the same vein, the Barbados Holidays with Pay Act gives the employer and the employee considerable leeway to negotiate on its practical application (Blackman, 1997, pp. 13–14). This type of legal flexibility also shows one important aspect of the interplay between legislation and collective bargaining: collective bargaining becomes a key means of giving effect to the legislation.

Collective bargaining

Collective agreements

Collective bargaining is clearly one of the main means of introducing labour market flexibility, and its role in doing so is the main theme of Chapters 3 and 5. This section briefly discusses the function of collective agreements as a means of industrial regulation and as a source of labour market flexibility.

For the purposes of this section, the term "collective agreement" is taken in its widest sense, from a single plant-level accord negotiated by a trade union and an employer to a pact concluded within the context of an arrangement for national-level tripartite (or "tripartite plus")[7] consultation. It ranges from informal shop-

---

[6] It is largely open-ended, leaving the parties to collective agreements free to reach agreement (Vidmar, 1997, pp. 9 and 28-32 for details on the Working Time Act 1982). With the 1970 reform, Swedish legislation dropped a reference to daily working hours (no longer seen as necessary) and provided for distribution of weekly hours over several weeks; the law was made no longer compulsory since a central agreement could override it. The legislation permits local agreements as well, and empowers the authorities to provide for exceptions to the rules even if no collective agreement is reached (ibid., pp.20, 28).

[7] "Tripartite plus" refers to involvement of representatives of civil society (e.g. consumers, environmental associations, cooperatives, women's groups, etc.) in consultative arrangements encompassing government and employers' and workers' representatives. See A. Trebilcock et al.: *Towards social dialogue: Tripartite cooperation in national economic and social policy-making* (ILO, 1994), pp. 35-36 and 51-63.

floor bargaining over issues such as overtime scheduling and job rotation to formal agreements among government, and employers' and workers' organizations concerning complex national pension schemes. Where high-level tripartite consultations produce negotiated outcomes, the process is often referred to as "social dialogue". Collective agreements can be both a means of amplifying or modifying the application of rights already guaranteed by law and a direct source of regulation on topics that are not completely addressed by legislation. In both cases, they set parameters for governance of the labour relationship as determined by the parties themselves (Windmuller, 1987, p. 3). Where the law does not impose restrictions, the parties to the agreements shape the content and the duration of an accord, and often the means by which a dispute may be resolved in the first instance. Work rules or codes of conduct effectively negotiated with management may also be seen as part of the collective bargaining system, but more often such rules and codes are unilaterally determined by the employer.

The idea of industrial democracy is inherent in collective bargaining, since it automatically involves a shift from unilateral to bilateral decision-making and usually involves procedures requiring a mandate from the membership.[8] The process culminating in a collective agreement can also elicit consent from those who live under its terms. Collective bargaining is an ongoing and open-ended process. It permits negotiation of "flexible arrangements which suit both employers and employees" (United Kingdom country study). As an illustration, a 1995 study in Ireland found that a greater percentage of jobs in all categories, especially manual and clerical, had become wider and more flexible in unionized firms as compared with non-union firms (Cranfield School of Management, 1996, cited in the Ireland country study). Denmark has also displayed a clear continuing preference for regulating labour relations and the employment relationship by means of collective agreements (van Peipje, 1998, pp. 204–205).

Collective bargaining is especially appropriate when legislation on a subject cannot be sufficiently detailed or exhaustive. Hours of work and the use of overtime have for this reason been an important subject of collective bargaining (Venezuela country study). With different rules for various sectors, collective agreements in Sweden provide considerable working-time flexibility (Vidmar, 1997, pp. 30–31). In Ireland, collective bargaining rather than legislation governs questions such as Sunday work, shift arrangements, minimum hours in the contract, payment for posts of responsibility, access to grievance procedures, and so on (Ireland country study).

---

[8] These range from the election of bargaining representatives to requirements laid down in trade union constitutions for the ratification, by a certain majority of the membership, of agreements negotiated by union representatives before they can enter into force.

In the past, collective agreements were traditionally based on expanding protection or extending entitlements. They still have that objective wherever possible, but sometimes cede ground under the pressure of contemporary economic trends (concession bargaining). While criticized in some quarters, this is also a testimony to the extreme flexibility of collective bargaining as a process. The Netherlands offers a prime example of industry-level agreements that have radically transformed the parameters of bargaining structures, work organization, working time, and the relationship between works councils and collective bargaining (Huiskamp, 1998, pp. 143-150). At the same time, the "pacifying function of collective agreements supports stability in a system of industrial relations" (van Peipje, 1998, pp. 202-203).

The interplay between collective bargaining and legislation

Collective bargaining and legislation often have a synergy that is expressed in several ways. Legislation can explicitly foresee a role for collective bargaining, with collective agreements becoming a means of implementing legislation. Such agreements can also act as a "corrective" measure where deregulatory legislation has pulled back to such an extent that it has left a void in workplace governance. And importantly, collective bargaining can also pave the way for legislation, either by pioneering innovative approaches or by forging a consensus that is needed for legislative reform. Thus, while legislation and collective bargaining retain their innate differences, they are often complementary as instruments of introducing flexibility measures. This is largely because the State plays a key role in labour relations, either by its action or its apparent inaction. The interrelationship between law and collective bargaining can even be expressed in constitutional terms, as in Brazil, which provides basic protections in relation to wages and hours of work, as well as escape clauses permitting derogations by means of collective agreements. Substantial use has been made of this possibility in regard to working hours (Brazil country study).

The role of the law is determinative in labour relations systems which permit the extension of collective agreements. The extent of coverage of a collective agreement can be legally affected in basically two ways. Even in a system considered as individualized or decentralized, the law can operate in such a way that a collective agreement may be enforceable in relation to non-members of an employer's organization and/or a trade union if the parties to it have so agreed. This case is illustrated by agreements in the United States motor industry, which provide that they apply to all non-probationary employees in the bargaining unit for which the agreement was negotiated, whether or not they are members of the trade union that serves as their exclusive bargaining representative. In countries with a more collectivist approach to labour relations, the law may go considerably further, by establishing a legal mechanism whereby the Government can order that a collective agreement be extended beyond its original confines. In the Netherlands, for example, the Minister of Social Affairs and Employment may declare all or parts of a collective agreement binding on an entire industry if he or she thinks that a significant majority of the employers and workers are already covered by the agreement. The extension is made only at the request of one of the parties to the agreement, and following consultation with the bipartite Labour Foundation.

In South Africa, an order extending the application of a collective agreement to non-parties may be issued if the most representative employers' organization and trade unions within the registered scope of the bargaining council favour the extension; the collective agreement itself must provide a mechanism for exemptions to be granted to non-parties. There is also separate provision for the Minister of Labour to extend the collective agreement if the parties are found to be sufficiently representative within the scope of the bargaining council, and the Minister finds that the failure to extend the agreement may undermine collective bargaining at the sectoral level.

Through such devices, as well as others, the scope of collective bargaining may be extended by law. Indeed, in countries such as France, Italy and Spain, the law plays a crucial role in making collective agreements applicable on such a broad scale.

Moreover, collective bargaining can lay the groundwork for legislation. To take one example, Italy's tripartite agreements have hammered out positions that permit reforming the law; such as abolishing the monopoly system of public placement or authorizing private agencies, with an active role for joint union-employer bodies. "Without the support of the social partners, this reform (Act No. 196 of 1997 on private agencies) would have been unthinkable" (Italy country study). The law itself is written in a way that builds in a role for collective bargaining.

While legislative reform in Spain was a precondition to introducing change in the labour market, it was not enough. It also produced a reaction provoked by the massive move to temporary contracts (96 per cent of contracts in 1996 were for three months or less) (Spain country study). The Interconfederational Agreement of 7 April 1997 was key to pursuing flexibility based on consensus. This three-part pact covers security of employment, collective bargaining and coverage of non-regulated subjects (to fill a gap left by the detailed labour ordinances of the Franco era, which were repealed). The new approach in Spain shows a synergy between the law and collective bargaining. For instance, the law (RDL 8/97) sets out a new framework for "training contracts" (*"contrato de formación"* or *"contrato en prácticas"*). The law did not change much substantively, but it permits collective agreements at various levels to determine the posts, groups, levels and occupational categories to which they apply, as well as (lower) rates to be paid. In the public sector, collective agreements can determine the number of training contracts and the jobs to which they apply (Spain country study).

Legislation can also be the outcome of an institutionalized social dialogue process. An important example of this occurs within the EU, where under the Protocol on Social Policy, the EC has established a two-step consultation process when it formulates proposals in the social policy field. The social partners are given a chance to reach a European-level agreement on an issue, and their solution can replace the Commission's proposal. Their negotiated compromise can be adopted by the European Council as a Directive, binding on all the Member States. "As a consequence of this legal innovation ... the social partners have obtained a status similar to quasi legislators" (Keller and Soerries, 1997, p. 20). The peak-level workers' and employers' representatives in the EU have reached accords which have eventually become EU Directives on part-time work and on parental leave.

At the national level, in Ireland, legally binding pay and conditions for all employers in the sectors covered are negotiated in joint labour committees, composed of employers, unions and an independent chair, and are then incorporated into employment regulation orders by the Government (Ireland country study). This dynamic relationship between collective bargaining and legislation can occur even in countries where there has not been a tradition of social dialogue. In the Republic of Korea, for instance, the successes and failures of the national negotiations among the Government, the employers and the two trade union federations in 1993–94 paved the way for labour law reform in 1996. The new law contains provisions encouraging "negotiated flexibility" by stipulating either consultation or agreement with the union or workers' representatives to introduce flexibility measures, including chiefly around working-hours issues (Republic of Korea country study).

The greater emphasis today on the role of the individual and his or her "employability" does not need to mean the abandonment of either labour legislation or collective bargaining. Ideally these mechanisms are still needed to compensate for the insufficient capacity for action that individuals display. When well conceived, the rules set down in legislation and in collective agreements should put the worker in a position of expressing and defending his or her individual interests in the context of a more competitive environment (Simitis, 1997, p. 665). As an instrument that can be shaped by the parties to meet their needs, collective bargaining affords a great opportunity to set parameters for flexibility that at once promote efficiency and equity.

Individual contracts of employment

Up to now, factors operating at the macro level – legislation and collective bargaining – have been reviewed in this chapter. However, the day-to-day experiences of workers and employers will also be significantly determined by the ways in which the employer exercises managerial prerogatives, and by the terms of the employment contract concluded by the employer and the employee. The importance of this relationship is being increasingly stressed by scholars: "The employment relationship as a distinct concept offers better opportunities for understanding developments in the nature of work, in the relationship between the market and the organization, and in the expectations and meanings of individual employees" (Huiskamp, 1998, pp. 148-149).

For the purpose of this study, two main issues are involved: the type of contract (flexibility of labour market entry) linking an enterprise and a worker, and the rules governing termination of the contractual relationship (flexibility of labour market exit). The first and most basic question is whether there is a "labour" relationship between a worker and an employer. The most significant development in relation to flexibility lies in the legal rules governing this question, and in employers' unilateral action to hive off certain aspects of their business as non-core activities, to conclude contracts with cooperatives and other entities composed of former employees, and to resort to other devices, including establishing new categories of contracts that escape the grasp of labour legislation (Brazil country study). A reduction in the employer's responsibility inevitably ends up rebounding upon the State (Simitis, 1997, p. 663), as well as society as a whole, in terms of providing social safety nets.

Existence of a contract of employment

As shown in Chapter 1, pressure is growing to develop other relationships involving the performance of work that may not always result in a contract of employment. The first question about these relationships as a source of flexibility is thus whether a classic employment relationship exists or not. If it does not, a maximum of flexibility, with a minimum of protection and a low level of legal predictability, will have been achieved. Obviously, contracts of employment can be a source of law only for those recognized as having them. Some new categories of workers are in fact engaged in disguised employment relationships, and the courts in most countries will examine whether or not a person is an employee regardless of the terms of the contract into which he or she has entered. Others present new paradigms, often in triangular or chain relationships, that elude regulation. Still others are relationships that would normally be designated as contracts of employment (employment promotion contracts, training contracts, new forms of apprenticeship, contracts for transition back into the labour market, and so on) but for political reasons have been designated otherwise so as to avoid certain legal consequences (for example, pension coverage) (Spain, in Veneziani, 1992, p. 35), or a regular minimum wage (Peru in the Peru country study). One author has called these slippery categories "employment on the borderline between independence and employment" (Mückenberger, in Veneziani, 1992, p. 240): first, forms escaping from labour and social security law by choosing contractual terms other than those of contracts of employment; second, forms attributable to job-creation activities of the State. Others involve persons who are genuinely self-employed, but who would improve their position if they were organized to defend their interests.

As Betten (1995) has observed, "A central role in changing industrial relations is played by the contract of employment which is seen as an instrument to protect part of the working population against, in general terms, unfair treatment ... (p. 3). The question is not the abolition of the contract of employment, but of rethinking its role and functioning in the context of transforming labour relations" (ibid., p. 4). A study of contracts of employment in seven developed countries concluded that, "the concept of 'personal subordination' may no longer be satisfactory as the determinant for affording persons in an employment relationship with a certain protection against, e.g. unfair termination of the contract. ...the time may have come to replace this notion with that of 'economic dependency'" (ibid., p. 7).

In the nineteenth century, it was seen as progress to move from the idea of status to a contractual framework (Browne, 1997, p. 24). While this was of course true where the status was medieval in nature (i.e. serfdom by virtue of birth), perhaps a new idea of status could help move forward the question of protecting all persons who perform work, whether they are in a formal employment relationship or not. The contract of employment emerged based on a paradigm of unity of time, place and activity. Traditional elements defining a contract of employment are an agreement on the performance of work, for remuneration, and above all involving the worker's dependency on or subordination to the employer. The legislator has grafted onto this a notion of continuity of employment as a precondition for entitlement to the various types of protection (social security, non-dismissal, and so on) (Veneziani, in Blanpain, 1990, p. 63). The challenge now facing labour law is how to come to grips with the new categories of "worker" which do not fit within the classic definition of "employee".

The very existence of these new forms of contractual arrangements exerts pressure on workers engaged under standard contracts of employment. The impact of such precarious contracts may be blunted by the fact that some people covered by them are protected by virtue of their dependency upon another person who enjoys full protection, such as a young person with a training contract who is still under the health-care protection of a parent, or a contract worker who is married to a person with a "regular" job that accrues pension rights, paid sick leave, and so forth. "...[W]ork relationships lie along a very broad spectrum of integration or dependency. ... In this rather complex universe, it seems rather simplistic to attempt to operate with two exclusive stereotypes. A more adequate response to these complexities would be to regard the law of the contract of employment as much more broadly applicable across the spectrum of work relationships ... It would be necessary to identify a category of dependent employment relationships for the purposes of various statutory regimes ...". (Freedland, quoted in Betten, 1995, pp. 22, 23).

The contract of employment as an instrument for introducing flexibility

Today, however, most individual employment relationships still do translate into contracts of employment, whether express or implied, and they can be a source of flexibility. But the contract of employment cannot be seen as a source or instrument on the same plane as legislation or collective bargaining. While influenced by law, and perhaps by collective agreements, a contract of employment is an undertaking between an individual and his or her employer. It gives rise to legally enforceable rights and obligations. For its effect, it relies not only on the parties' honouring it, but on what the legal system of a country offers in terms of general rules and means of enforcement when one of the parties does not. Thus a contract of employment on its own is not backed up by the collective will that legislation expresses or the potential of mass action that collectively bargained agreements harbour. As Betten (1995, p. 7) concluded about Europe, "[T]he influence on the contents of the employment contract by the individual parties involved is very minor ... the effect of working conditions agreed to at a collective level remains predominant". Given the potential for exploitation of the weaker party, that is fortunate. A study of the effect of the Employment Contracts Act in New Zealand showed that "employee concessions during the formation of new contracts were significantly more likely under individual contracts than under collective contracts" (McAndrew, 1992, cited in the New Zealand country study).

The view of Kahn Freund and Wedderburn, noted labour scholars, that the imbalance of power between a worker and an employer implies that the contract of employment represents only a fiction of a real agreement based on meaningful negotiations, still seems valid. The vulnerability of individual workers is obviously enhanced by increased mobility of capital, high unemployment rates and other factors outside their control. Thus while contracts of employment are concluded freely by individuals, they are subject to legal restrictions. The legal parameters involve the types of contracts permitted, their content and the means of resolving disputes over their interpretation and enforcement. As a general rule, an individual contract of employment may deviate from legislation or a collective agreement only to the extent that it provides an arrangement more favourable to the employee (Italy country study). Where individual agreement can permit a derogation from the law, this will often be turned into employers' unilateral action.

It is with regard to contracts of employment that the differing mind-sets of civil and common law are perhaps most clearly revealed. In common-law countries, the contract of employment is subject above all to the judge-made rules that created it, albeit often varied (not determined) by legislation (Ireland country study) and with shifting analyses and tests used over time (Browne, 1997, pp. 23–27). Thus flexibility already exists at the heart of the contract under common law, and resort to fixed-term contracts or contracts for part-time work, for instance, would not be excluded except by legislation. With the influence of EU membership, the role of legislation in the employment relationship has developed significantly in Ireland and the United Kingdom; the same cannot be said for non-European countries inspired by the common law of England, however, which still follow the "employment at will" doctrine except to the extent modified by legislation.

There exist in law various types of employment contract – "open-ended" contracts without limit of time, fixed-term contracts, and so forth. However, the parties' freedom of contract is limited in many European countries by restrictions on the conclusion of fixed-term contracts. They are made subject to particular requirements, and there is sometimes a ban on their renewal or a limitation on the number of renewals possible (in France, Belgium, Netherlands, Portugal, Italy and Spain) (Veneziani, 1992, p. 33). In some systems, the exceptional nature of fixed-term contracts is shown by the requirement that they be in writing, thus being explicit derogations from rules normally regulating the labour relationship (ibid., pp. 31 and 93). This idea is reflected in the EC Directive of 1991 on information which must be contained in the employment contract in writing.

Denmark does not legislatively regulate contracts of employment (Veneziani, 1992), but collective bargaining has ensured important guarantees in regard to the terms and conditions of employment for individual workers. As in a number of other European countries, the legislation contains a "corrective" protection: an unjustified renewal of a series of fixed-term contracts leads to transformation into a permanent contract (ibid., p. 33). Similarly, Japanese law creates a restriction in relation to contracts of employment: they must either be up to one year or unlimited (Japan country study). The type of contract – fixed-term, without limit of time, and so on – is often determinative when it comes to termination of employment, it being most difficult to end the employment relationship with worker under a contract for an unlimited term.

At the other end of the spectrum, the probationary period provided by law or by individual or collective agreement builds in flexibility as regards termination by either party at the outset of the relationship. The existence of the probationary phase provides the parties with a useful trial period, as long as it is indeed used for that purpose (a reasonable period to test whether the worker is up to the job) rather than being subverted (by unreasonable length, by renewal of a series of so-called probationary periods, or by resort to a pool of revolving probationary workers to accomplish core work) to avoid entering into types of employment contracts that would afford greater protection.

There are countries in which contracts of employment play almost no role for most workers. For most of this century in Sweden, the individual contract of employment has had only one variable term for manual workers (its date of commencement) and two for white-collar employees (the date and the starting pay) (Betten, 1995, p. 91); all the rest of the terms derive from other sources. "The employer prerogatives limit the role of employment contracts since most of the terrain for individual employment regulation is already occupied by unilateral employer authority" (ibid., p. 83). Terms will often be implied in contracts of employment. For instance, the Supreme Court of Japan has held that provisions in employer-determined work rules, if reasonable, are incorporated into individual contracts of employment (ibid., p. 113).

The implications of factors such as the ascendancy of free-market ideologies, the adoption of human resource management techniques that stress the role of individual interests over the collective interests of the workforce, and the increase in small businesses which do not lend themselves as easily as larger ones to collective labour relations, all suggest that the role of the individual contract of employment may be growing (ibid., p. 158). To this must be added the growth of alternative forms of contractual arrangements outside the "typical" model of full-time employment at the workplace of a single employer. The growing phenomenon in many countries of inventing alternatives to the contract of employment, with the effect of depriving workers of the protection afforded by virtue of employee status, has important implications for the extent of protection, if any, that workers may enjoy while performing work. Exercising free will is a fundamental freedom, but legislation and collective bargaining have important roles to play in ensuring that workers do not agree to any and all terms and conditions of employment, and that employers do not get bogged down by time-consuming one-to-one dealings with their workforce. In a period when, in many countries, collective means of representation have lost ground, it does not make sense to look to an individual relationship that involves the worker's inherent vulnerability as a preferred method for introducing flexibility measures.

Employers' unilateral action

The term "employers' unilateral action" needs to be defined in relation to the level of action being taken. At the highest level of the enterprise, decision-making on strategy about what goods or services to produce or provide, and where to do so, falls clearly within the ambit of unilateral action of the employer in free market economies. Some firms of course have provision for employees' involvement on boards of directors, but this does not change the fact that ultimate responsibility for major business decisions lies with those who own the company. In many countries, court decisions have been a vehicle for stating what are considered to be managerial prerogatives, sometimes referred to as "management rights". Questions of self-organization of the operation and employees' tenure (hiring and termination) lie at the heart of these. There is also a need to distinguish between the powers of "employers" when one speaks of either the owners of a business or a local manager who is to carry out the policy of a large company. When the term "employers' unilateral action" refers to shop-floor practices, however, there may well be more give and take between management and workers than would be indicated by an organizational chart of the firm.

Unilateral action by the employer is probably the most important source of flexibility, exercised both directly and indirectly. Direct exercise comes in organizing work, laying down rules and giving instructions or orders. There are also great differences in the manner in which an employer exerts unilateral decision making. In hierarchical, Taylorist work organization settings, the supervisor operates with coercive power. In more modern work settings, management uses its authority and leadership to introduce participatory practices such as teamwork, quality circles and the like. Indirect unilateral action involves exerting pressure to obtain consent, as through a workers' participation scheme, or in discussions for concluding an employment contract. In relation to contracts of employment, a New Zealand court has observed that the time for exercising management prerogatives is when entering into such a contract (New Zealand country study). In Brazil unilateral action has been used to introduce wage cuts, changes in working hours, work assignments, work organization and even the relationship (from employer/employee to a third-party arrangement). Even when this is disguised as an individual or pluri-individual agreement, it essentially involves unilateral action by the dominant party, that is, the employer (Brazil country study).

Work rules may be negotiated, but often they are a source of regulation that derives from unilateral employer action. That remains true even when consultation on the rules is required, since the ultimate decision still rests with the employer. Traditionally, work rules have been directed at the conduct of individual workers, rather than institutional arrangements. However, to the extent that they impinge on areas such as proper occupational safety and health practices, they may touch on issues of work organization that affect the body of workers and first-line managers. The legal effect of work rules differs by country, but sometimes a statute will specify that they cannot conflict with the terms of an applicable collective agreement (Republic of Korea country study). The Labour Standards Act of Japan 1947 requires enterprises employing ten or more workers to adopt work rules, which are filed with the labour inspectorate. Many Latin American countries also have legislatively mandated work rules at the enterprise level. Contemporary management theory plays down work rules in favour of other means of influencing employees' behaviour, however, such as participation schemes, incentives and teamwork.

Managers have a wide range of choice about the type of strategy they choose to employ when it comes to adopting flexibility measures. In the newly deregulated context of Australia, it appears that when introducing change, employers still rely heavily on consultation with employees when there is no employee representation (Australia country study). Employers will resort to unilateral action where they think that trade union representatives are too slow in responding or when they are refusing to agree on the essence of what management seeks. Some managers feel that the collective bargaining process sits uneasily with the demands of flexibility in a complicated world (United Kingdom country study). Yet the fact remains that employers have a choice between exercising their managerial prerogatives in a manner which either provokes confrontation or promotes cooperation. When it comes to introducing flexibility measures that will depend on employees' cooperation for their success, the latter approach is clearly to be preferred.

The State has an important role to play in determining the relative weight that legislation, collective bargaining, contracts of employment and unilateral action by employers will be given in a country in any chosen period. With the ILO's member States having recently renewed a pledge "to respect, to promote and to realize" the principles and rights relating to "the effective recognition of the right to collective bargaining" (ILO Declaration on Fundamental Principles and Rights at Work and its Follow-up, 1998, para. 2(a)), state action could set the framework for preferring collective bargaining as a means of addressing changing circumstances in the world of work.

THE ROLE OF THE STATE AND THE BARGAINING STRUCTURE

3

Introduction

The globalization of economies is imposing unprecedented constraints on the autonomous capacity of the national social partners to determine their own destiny. As the ILO's *World Labour Report 1997–98* describes, high capital mobility has contributed to the shrinking autonomy of national products and labour markets, as well as public policy setting. At the same time, the autonomy of the enterprise is increasing (ILO, 1997, p. 82). Consequently, the role of the State and the social partners in the labour market and industrial relations has been subject to huge pressures for change. The decentralization of industrial relations, especially collective bargaining, along with the deregulation of labour markets, have often gone hand in hand with labour market flexibilization – although there has also been evidence of a recentralization taking place in certain countries as well. This chapter examines the recent changes in the role of the State as an actor in industrial relations, as well as the adaptation of the structures of collective bargaining to increasing labour market flexibility.

While governments in some countries – particularly those which pursue neo-liberal economic policies – have withdrawn from active intervention in industrial relations over the past decade, other countries have begun to engage more extensively in tripartite consultations. In the following sections, we review recent developments in four groups of countries: industrialized countries with "voluntarist" industrial relations; continental European countries; Central and Latin American countries; and Asian countries.

In European countries with a long tradition of social dialogue at levels above the enterprise, governments and higher-level collective bargaining continue to play a crucial role in the labour market. These countries have maintained relatively centralized decision-making structures in which consultation and negotiation play the largest possible role. As regards designing and implementing economic and social policies, these countries have tried to associate – rather than disassociate – the action of the public authorities and the social partners. However, it should be noted that globalization has posed a serious threat to the "corporatist" strategies pursued by some European countries by undermining the socioeconomic foundation of the social pact which followed the Second World War.

In Latin American countries, where the State has traditionally played a protectionist role in individual labour relations while limiting collective bargaining's role in the labour market, governments are increasingly taking drastic measures to dismantle labour market regulations through legislative changes. As the role of collective bargaining at various levels has been quite limited to date, a kind of institutional vacuum is now apparent.

Asia has shown considerable diversity in its approach to industrial relations and labour market change: a partial attempt to move away from the State's repressive intervention in both the labour market and industrial relations towards labour market deregulation through tripartite and bipartite negotiation (the Republic of Korea); non-active involvement of the State in labour market affairs in the context of the ineffectiveness of collective bargaining to influence labour market flexibility (India and the Philippines); and the continuing importance of labour-management cooperation at the enterprise level and informal coordination with the Government's indirect involvement at the higher level (Japan).

Industrialized countries with "voluntarist" industrial relations

In countries such as Australia, Canada, New Zealand, the United Kingdom and the United States, which share common law tradition, the State has either not been a party in the collective bargaining process, or has recently tended to withdraw from industrial relations. Thus, industrial relations in these countries today can be characterized as "voluntarist", in that the State does not play an active role, leaving employers and trade unions largely free to determine employment conditions, as well as the patterns of their mutual relationship.

However, there is considerable variation in the tradition of industrial relations among these countries. For example, until recently, state intervention in determining employment conditions through arbitration tribunals was the main feature of industry relations in Australia and New Zealand. In Canada, tripartite consultations at the national and industrial levels have recently been playing a role in the social and economic decision-making process, and in creating a sound basis for the smooth operation of the industrial relations system. An example of such tripartite dealings is the so-called "Social Contract" concluded in Quebec at the joint initiative of unions and employers, but with the support of the provincial government. The Social Contract includes no-strike pledges for periods of up to eight years, in return for a commitment by employers to invest in creating jobs or at least in preserving them (Melz and Verma, 1995, p. 116). The United Kingdom and the United States have traditionally had highly voluntaristic systems of industrial relations, in which the Government has refrained from taking part. However, there are important differences between these two countries. The process of collective bargaining in the United States is extensively regulated by the National Labor Relations Act 1935, which provides for the determination of bargaining units and the certification of exclusive bargaining agents, and establishes the duty to bargain, mainly revolving around the definition of mandatory and permissible subjects for bargaining. In the United Kingdom, there is no close equivalent to such detailed regulation, although it is true that the 1980s witnessed an upsurge in the regulation of industrial relations, particularly those governing union behaviour.

As to the bargaining structure, the countries in this group share a common feature – a structure that is generally more decentralized than in most other industrialized countries, particularly those in continental Europe. Yet there is also some inter-country variation. For example, although the United States and Canada have traditionally had decentralized collective bargaining, there is evidence that it is being further decentralized. In the United States, "pattern bargaining" has disappeared from all but a few select industries. A similar trend may also be observed in Canada, although to a lesser extent. In the United Kingdom, decentralization has taken the form of the demise of industry-wide agreements (ILO, 1997, pp. 113–114). In Australia and New Zealand, where centralized arbitration and awards have played a crucial role in collective bargaining, drastic decentralization occurred in different ways and at different paces. In Australia, decentralization has been a gradual process, in which employers' and workers' organizations have been closely involved, at least until recently. On the other hand, New Zealand has experienced a radical decentralization of collective bargaining following the enactment of the Employment Contracts Act in 1991.

Let us now examine more closely the differences in the process of change taking place in these countries. In the United States, although collective bargaining at the enterprise or plant level has always been prevalent, "pattern bargaining" was used to enable the application of relatively homogeneous conditions of employment to all unionized enterprises within a given sector, most notably the motor, steel and mining industries. Non-unionized enterprises – larger ones in particular – tended to apply comparable conditions to their employees, as they sought to recruit and retain high-quality workers and to preclude the establishment of trade unions within their firms; this contributed to extending the homogenization to non-union enterprises. However, with the deregulation policies pursued by the Government in the early 1980s, pattern bargaining has withered away in most sectors and, as a result, enterprise-level collective agreements have lost their main source of strength (ILO, 1997, p. 112).

While the weakening of "pattern bargaining" in Canada is also a clear sign of decentralization, bipartite and tripartite consultations play a significant role at the national and industrial levels, in contrast with the United States. For instance, industry-level joint committees like the Canadian Textile Labour Management Committee and the Canadian Steel Trade and Employment Congress, which were formed in 1967 and 1985 respectively, received renewed attention in the 1980s as a way of focusing on the mutual interests of labour and management (Meltz and Verma, 1995, p. 113). Also important in the 1980s were a number of private and public initiatives at the national level in which workers and employers tried to arrive at broad understandings. As examples of the outcomes of these initiatives, the following may be cited: the recommendations of the Advisory Council on Adjustment, which helped develop a national training policy in 1990; the labour-management joint report, *The search for a better way,* which spells out a code of conduct for labour-management relations and encourages the adoption of innovations at the firm level (ibid., 115); and the Social Contract of Quebec, mentioned earlier.

The policy of the successive Conservative Governments in the United Kingdom sought to lower the level of established rights and avoid the establishment of new minimum standards (United Kingdom country study). While trade unions have traditionally provided a substitute for legislative protection, they are no longer capable of doing so effectively, as they have been weakened by successive government attacks on them through legislation. Central negotiations and consultations, which have never played an important role in the United Kingdom, have virtually disappeared, as most central tripartite advisory bodies were abolished by the Government. In many industries, such as engineering, multi-employer agreements have been terminated altogether, while those in other industries merely set minimum terms which directly affect only a minority of employees. However, the accession of the Labour Party to power in 1997, and its advocacy of "partnership" in economic development, may lead to changes in the industrial relations climate. Be that as it may, the nature of collective bargaining in the United Kingdom offers considerable scope for further negotiation and/or adaptation in the enterprise and at the workplace. The form of higher-level agreements in the country provides ample room for the social partners at lower levels to maximize flexibility. Thus, whether the lower-level parties have the ability to reach an acceptable agreement tends to set the practical limits to the process.

The most extreme decentralization of collective bargaining occurred in New Zealand, where the National Party Government, strongly believing in the effectiveness of free markets, introduced changes which go further than those introduced by the British Conservative Government. Although the need for labour market flexibility, in particular the need to move away from an occupationally based award system, was recognized by all social partners as early as the mid-1980s, several attempts in the second half of the 1980s to reform the industrial relations system (e.g. the Labour Relations Act 1987) failed, owing to conflicting views among the social partners on the desirable direction of the changes. In the meantime, the deregulation of the goods and services markets and trade liberalization measures have intensified pressures to flexibilize the labour market.

Under New Zealand's Employment Contracts Act 1991, there was a dramatic shift from multi-employer bargaining to enterprise bargaining. In May 1991, 50 per cent of employees in the private sector were covered by multi-employer settlements; by August 1992 this figure had fallen dramatically to 9 per cent; a year later, it had dropped even further to 6 per cent. While 77 per cent of the agreements concluded in 1989–90 were multi-employer agreements, 80 per cent of those entered into in 1994–95 were single-enterprise agreements (Harbridge and Honeybone, 1996, cited in the New Zealand country study). In some cases, the decentralization process went even further, and ended up in the substitution of individual contracts for collective agreements.

These changes in the bargaining structure also affect the methods of wage determination in New Zealand. The previous multi-tiered wage-determination system has been replaced by decentralized enterprise bargaining, constrained only by minimum-wage legislation. The Employment Contracts Act has explicitly withdrawn all exclusive rights previously accorded to unions in labour market regulation. For example, the issue of whether bargaining is to be towards individual or collective employment contracts is itself a matter for negotiation, the primary parties to such negotiation being the individual employee and his or her employer.

In Australia, until 1996 the decentralization of collective bargaining was implemented through close cooperation between the federal Labor Government and the Australian Council of Trade Unions (ACTU). The ACTU endorsed a shift from the centralized system of bargaining to a more decentralized system in which enterprise-level bargaining plays a role in enhancing enterprise flexibility, while the award system continues to play a protective role. It also endorsed the devolution of many functions it used to carry out to unions at the workplace. This shift did not mean, however, that the ACTU gave up its prominent role in shaping bargaining and wage policies within the framework of "the Accords", which stressed negotiations over social and economic priorities and policies. Unions at the enterprise level, however, have had some difficulties in exercising the kind of leverage that was available to the ACTU through its national power base, because they have not traditionally been well organized in the workplace. In practice, the vast majority of agreements were negotiated as adjustments to awards, while in theory, enterprise agreements were expected to replace awards. The devolution of labour power to the firm level appears to have hampered the diffusion of workplace reforms through enterprise negotiation because of the weak union base (Wever, 1997, p. 463).

The pace of decentralization has been accelerated by the election of the federal Liberal and National Coalition Government, bringing an end to "Australian-style corporatism". Negotiations at the national level between the Government and the ACTU have come to an end, implying that the only level for bargaining over flexibility is now at the enterprise. In addition, the Workplace Relations Act 1996 expanded the possibility for individual bargaining and non-union collective agreements. The Coalition Government has not attempted to provide any forum for nationwide negotiations to replace the Accords (Australia country study).

European countries with a tradition of social partnership

In European countries where centralized bargaining and social partnerships have been the prominent features of their social and economic systems, there have been growing pressures for change given the globalization of the economy and the consequent drive towards labour market flexibility. As elsewhere, the enterprise is becoming an important level of collective bargaining, while centralized collective bargaining systems are experiencing difficulties in adapting themselves to this new reality. Governments, in regulating labour markets, have had similar difficulties in coping with record high unemployment and the need for labour market flexibility. However, the ways in which the role of the State and the bargaining structures in these European countries are changing are not the same as in those countries with "voluntarist" industrial relations, discussed in the preceding section. While the enterprise is assuming growing importance in collective bargaining and industrial relations, collective bargaining at the national and industrial levels in most continental European countries and in Ireland still plays an important role as a means of establishing the framework for negotiations at the enterprise level. Moreover, the governments in these European countries have generally shown a clear commitment to social partnership in pursuing labour market flexibility. In some cases, they show such commitment through their participation in tripartite negotiations, or by supporting bipartite negotiations. At times, they intervene more directly in the labour market in order to make up for the weaknesses of collective bargaining.

The role of the State

The need for labour market flexibility and the evolving structure of collective bargaining have called for a changing role of the State in European countries. The emergence of new forms of work which are hardly covered by existing State regulations, and the greater emphasis on the enterprise as a crucial unit for change have inevitably urged a new role for the State. However, the direction of such changes differs substantially by country.

Although decentralized collective bargaining is often said to be more instrumental than centralized collective bargaining in promoting labour market flexibility, some governments have been able to achieve a degree of economic growth and macroeconomic stability by actively supporting centralized collective bargaining. This is the case in Ireland and Norway, where the relative success of these countries in both economic growth and employment creation has been largely due to their broadly set incomes policies, called the "Solidarity Alternative" in Norway and the "Programme for National Recovery" (PNR) in Ireland. Both parties in industry have actively participated in formulating these policies. Centralized collective bargaining in each country delivered moderate wage increases, and enabled relatively high economic growth – and hence job creation. There seems to be wide consensus that the system of social partnership is at the root of the economic success which both countries have enjoyed for some years now.

In particular, the move towards "bargained corporatism" or a "system of social partnership" in Ireland, where the common law system granted few rights to employees, has accompanied new legislative initiatives by the Government aimed at extending elements of the floor of rights enshrined in employment legislation to temporary, part-time and agency workers. The extension of the regulatory framework has been intrinsically bound up with national bargaining. In general, however, the Irish Government "allowed the issues of functional, numerical or temporal flexibility to be determined by employers or negotiated at the local level between the social partners" (Ireland country study).

In countries such as Spain and the Netherlands, the State's role in labour market regulations has diminished. In the Netherlands, for example, where the Government traditionally has exerted an unusual degree of influence on industrial relations and the labour market, it has increasingly given employers and workers greater responsibility for determining employment conditions. The new Working Time Act 1996 (*Arbeidstijdenwet*, or ATW), which largely replaces the Labour Act 1919 (*Arbeidswet*, or AW), is an explicit reflection of current developments in Dutch industrial relations. The ATW aims to give much more scope to the social partners for self-regulation of working time matters, through the "consultation regulation", though within certain limits. Furthermore, it gives works councils and trade unions a role in monitoring and controlling working time, as well as in determining it (the Netherlands country study). The same principle is applied to wage determination. While the wage-determination process in the 1970s had been marked by active government intervention through pay guidelines and pay freezes, decentralization has been achieved through a partial government retreat from the process as a result of a 1987 amendment to Article 10 of the Wage Determination Act 1970. Until now, the Government has stimulated the development of programmes for profit sharing and share ownership by fiscal means.

In France, on the other hand, where the role of collective bargaining has been less crucial than in other European countries, the Government has continued to use administrative measures to induce bipartite negotiations on labour market flexibility. In 1993, it decided to grant a 30 per cent tax cut to enterprises which transform full-time workers to part-time workers, provided they maintain the same level of total working hours. To support this policy, it ensured that the same rights that full-time workers normally enjoy would be granted to part-time workers. As a way of reducing unemployment, the Government began to offer fiscal incentives of tax cuts for employers and unions, if both parties reached collective agreements to reduce working time by at least 19 per cent in order to either preserve 10 per cent of existing jobs or create an additional 10 per cent new jobs.

If central consultations or negoiations fail in spite of all government efforts, the public authorities often impose their views on employers and workers through legislation or other regulations. This was the case, for example, in Belgium where in 1993 the Government imposed the so-called "Global Plan" after central tripartite negotiations had failed. The Global Plan placed some restrictions on the traditional automatic wage indexation system and practically froze wages for three years. The Plan also included many detailed measures aimed at flexibilizing the labour market, reforming the social security system and, protecting and creating employment. In 1996, the failure of tripartite negotiations led to the promulgation of several framework laws, among them ones on wage fixing and employment creation. These framework laws provide that if the parties cannot agree on the issues concerned within a given time limit, the Government would have to impose a solution (for wage issues) or could impose a solution (for employment creation issues). In fact, the parties were unable to agree on anything for 1997, thus obliging the Government to impose its own decisions on wages, employment and other labour market issues.

In the majority of European countries with a tradition of social partnership, however, when the Government intervenes in industrial relations, it normally does not substitute for employers and workers in social regulation, but rather its role becomes closely intertwined with that of the social partners. This is not a new phenomenon. Collective bargaining has always been used in these countries as a means of working out ways in which legislation is applied, and adjusting it to the specific circumstances prevailing in the various sectors and enterprises. Moreover, collective bargaining has always played a role in preparing legislation to the extent that legislation is based on agreements between the central employers' and workers' organizations, or merely confirms solutions previously worked out and tested through major sectoral or enterprise agreements. What is new is that the interlinkage between the actions of the State and of the social partners has become even closer, and the potential synergy between them has been more fully exploited. This is because more and more issues can no longer be resolved without legislative change or without financial intervention by the State, and the State wishes to associate employers and workers with this process to the largest extent possible. Indeed, legislation today increasingly provides that less favourable conditions for the workers than those fixed in legislation can be applied at the sectoral or enterprise level, provided that this results from collective bargaining between representative partners. The Dutch Working Time Act (ATW), mentioned earlier, provides a good example of this recent trend.

In Italy, a major accord was signed in July 1993 between the Government, central trade unions and employers' organizations which symbolizes a consensus-based approach to labour market reform. The "Social Pact" was aimed at reforming collective bargaining, introducing flexibility into the labour market and establishing an incomes policy (this accord will be described in detail in Chapter 5). It represented a coordinated approach by the social partners to reshaping the "rules of the game" for industrial relations, by establishing the parameters within which bargaining should be conducted and policy formulated. The Italian Government has also been relying on the initiatives taken by the social partners, through bipartite collective bargaining, in regulating newly emerging forms of employment. As there is still no legal provision covering most of these forms of employment, they are often regulated on an experimental basis, first through collective bargaining at the enterprise level and then at the industry level. It was only after further bargaining experience on the issue that specific legal regulation was attempted. This approach was used to deal with temporary agency work, and led to its legitimization under the 1993 accord. Also, innovative experiments are being carried out in order to develop rules governing teleworking. Under Act N.300 of 1970, it is unlawful to use audiovisual and similar equipment for supervising and controlling employees at a distance. A collective agreement signed in August 1995 by Telecom Italia and its unions has led to the launching of a home teleworking project. It is anticipated that, after these experiments, new legislation governing teleworking will be prepared.

In Spain, where legislation has traditionally regulated the labour market quite rigidly, the social partners were at loggerheads with each other over the best way to introduce flexibility. In April 1997, they finally reached an interconfederal agreement and completed a series of labour market reforms which had been started in 1994 with the reform of the Workers' Statute (*Estatuto de los Trabajadores*). The agreement sought above all to strike an adequate balance among different forms of flexibility, and to enrich collective bargaining as a means of regulating working conditions (Spain country study). Tripartite consultations had mostly failed until 1996–97, when there was a breakthrough in negotiations on some specific issues, leading to the conclusion of a bipartite agreement on each of them separately. At the same time, the social partners agreed to broaden the agenda and deal with such delicate topics as the employers' demand to reduce severance/redundancy pay, and the unions' wish to discuss the future of the National Institute of Employment, and privatization. Significantly, even though discussions were conflictual, and were occasionally broken off, there was a willingness on both sides to continue negotiations until a set of balanced agreements could be reached. Among other things, the agreements set up a commission to monitor the effects of the reforms over a four-year period, and requested the Government to enact tax measures favouring the creation of permanent jobs. After obtaining the endorsement of the tripartite Economic and Social Council, the agreements were promulgated as a royal legislative decree in August 1997. The new legislation has taken into account the outcomes of bipartite negotiations and has promoted collective bargaining.

The level of collective bargaining

As has just been shown, collective bargaining at the central level is still playing an important role in many European countries with a tradition of social partnership. Higher-level bargaining sets the framework for negotiations at the enterprise level, and provides macroeconomic stability and consensus on a social agenda. Nevertheless, even in these countries, there is today a trend towards decentralization, notable not so much in the decline of central bargaining as in the growth of bargaining at the enterprise or workplace level. This is mainly because the search for greater labour market flexibility and higher competitiveness increasingly requires working out solutions to problems that are well adapted to the specific circumstances of the enterprise.

In France, since the mid-1980s, wage negotiations have been taking place increasingly at the enterprise level rather than at the sectoral level. The National Council of French Employers (CNPF) has supported this decentralization process, by abandoning in 1987 the practice of recommending a specific percentage wage increase to all private sector enterprises, and by ending in 1995 another practice of issuing annual wage policy recommendations. The increase in enterprise agreements confirm this trend, as their numbers rose from 6,496 in 1990 to 8,550 in 1995. In Germany, industry-wide agreements increasingly include an "opening clause" which allows works councils and employers to negotiate amendments to these agreements at the enterprise level. More recently, the agreement signed in the chemical industry in 1997 (discussed in more detail in Chapter 5) provided the possibility for enterprises to negotiate a variable portion of wages which may be increased or decreased according to the local economic situation. Agreements with an opening clause for lower-level negotiations have also been concluded recently in Austria and the Netherlands.

Central industrial relations have lost most ground in Sweden, where they traditionally played a very important role. Decentralization in this country has mainly consisted of the demise of central bipartite agreements and the collapse of the tripartite structure of various administrative boards. The first step towards decentralization was taken in 1983, when VF, the engineering employers' federation, broke away from central bargaining and concluded a separate agreement with the Metal Workers Union (Metall) and with the white-collar unions. After VF played a key role in changing the leadership, policy, and organization of the Swedish Employers' Confederation (SAF) in 1989, the SAF board formally declared that wage negotiations should henceforth take place only at the industry and company levels. Decentralization also occurred in the public sector, which involved a reduction of general pay increases through public service central negotiations and an increase in the amount apportioned to each administration/agency for distribution through workplace negotiation.

Despite the move to decentralization, enterprise bargaining in European countries is still rather limited. In 1995, enterprise agreements covered only 8 per cent of workers in the private sector in the Netherlands (compared to 75 per cent for industry-wide agreements), 14 per cent in Spain (about 70 per cent for industry-wide agreements), and 25 per cent in France (over 80 per cent for industry-wide agreements) (ILO, 1997, p. 120). Moreover, the importance of enterprise-level bargaining may be even smaller than these figures suggest. A recent study of the French metal sector reveals, for example, that while the number of enterprise agreements has considerably increased in recent years – partly due to the incentives provided for by legislation, and in central and sectoral agreements – the content and impact of these enterprise agreements are relatively poor (Gazon, 1995).

As a general rule, there is no dismantling of central industrial relations in European countries with a tradition of social partnership. Central industrial relations have clearly been weakened, but still play a significant role. The most visible signs of their growing weakness are the frequent failures of central consultations or negotiations – such as the experiences of Belgium in 1993 and 1996, and of Spain in 1993 and 1996 – as well as the inability of many recent central agreements to include precise provisions. As mentioned earlier, an increasing number of central agreements leave considerable room for manoeuvre to the parties at lower levels.

The recent experience of Belgium, referred to previously, illustrates the difficulties facing tripartite consultations and negotiations today. In this country, where collective bargaining had practically been suspended by the Government between 1981 and 1985 and closely supervised by it in the following years, the Prime Minister in 1993 proposed the conclusion of an ambitious Social Pact. The negotiations failed and, as a consequence, the Government imposed its views through a set of laws and regulations known as the Global Plan. When the Plan expired in 1996, the Government again proposed the conclusion of an ambitious tripartite agreement covering several years. This time, the negotiations succeeded, but the draft agreement was not ratified by the competent bodies of one of the important trade unions. This led the Government to pass a number of framework laws on wages and job creation measures.

In spite of the growing difficulties, however, tripartite consultations and negotiations are still practised, to varying degrees, in the countries where they have a strong tradition, as in Austria, the Netherlands and Ireland.

The Austrian system, which places greater emphasis on in-depth and regular consultation on major economic and social issues than on the conclusion of formal agreements, continues to function effectively. This is illustrated, for example, by the extensive tripartite consultations which took place in the process of preparing the 1996 Budget, and by the adoption in March 1996 of a detailed joint position of the central employers' and workers' organizations on matters relating to the future development of the EU. A little earlier, the viability of Austrian tripartism had been clearly demonstrated by the adoption, in 1992 and 1993 respectively, of a Declaration of Principle on Social Partnership (bipartite) and a Stability Pact (tripartite), both reflecting the social partners' concern that requirements arising from the globalization of the economy and Austria's accession to the EU should be taken into account in national policy making.

In the Netherlands, which underwent a period marked by serious economic and social difficulties in the late seventies and the early eighties, a milestone tripartite agreement – called the Wassenaar agreement – was signed in 1982, whereby employers and workers struck a trade-off between the standard of living (i.e. the level of wages and social benefits, including social security benefits) and job creation. This basic principle has underlain economic and social policy in the Netherlands since 1982, founded on continuous consultation and negotiation between the social partners, including the Government. The durability of the traditional social partnership in the Netherlands may be one of the main factors accounting for the country's recent success in reconciling the requirements of the competitiveness of the national economy with the "social" approach which has characterized economic and social policy in continental Western Europe.

In Ireland, initially bipartite and subsequently tripartite central negotiations took place throughout most of the seventies. After a return to decentralized bargaining between 1980 and 1987, there was a shift back to central tripartite bargaining after 1988. Since then, the partners have concluded four major agreements: the National Recovery Programme (1988–90); the Programme for Economic and Social Progress (1991–93); the Programme for Competitiveness and Work (1994–96); and Partnership 2000 (1997–99). These have enabled inflation and interest rates to remain low and the debt/GNP ratio to fall, while simultaneously achieving high economic growth and reducing unemployment, although it still remains high.

Elsewhere, central industrial relations have generally lost more ground than in Austria, the Netherlands and Ireland. In spite of these difficulties, however, central consultations and negotiations remain a key factor in the industrial relations systems of continental European countries. In Italy, for example, important central agreements were concluded in July 1992 and September 1996, in addition to the July 1993 agreement mentioned earlier. It should also be noted that central consultation and negotiation still play a key role in countries such as Denmark and Norway, where sectoral bargaining continues to be closely coordinated by central organizations. In Denmark, for example, sectoral employers' organizations must submit draft agreements for approval to the central employers' organization before signing them. This is not strictly pro forma, as approval has been withheld by the central organizations in certain instances. In other countries, such as Finland and Portugal, the past few years have witnessed a trend towards centralization of negotiations, although this trend may not be a lasting one. Indeed, in these two countries, central agreements were concluded in 1995 and 1996 respectively, following a period of several years without central bargaining.

Thus, although central consultation and negotiation have been subject to considerable difficulties and have experienced failures, there have more attempts at recourse to them in the 1990s than in previous decades. Indeed, in virtually all continental European countries, appeals have been made in recent years – usually by governments, but sometimes also by trade unions or employers' organizations – to conclude some sort of "social pact" to resolve burning social issues. This is true even of countries traditionally reluctant to engage in central industrial relations, such as Germany. While an attempt to conclude a country-wide tripartite "Pact for Employment" in 1995 failed in that country, it has nevertheless had a number of spin-offs: first, a country-wide agreement – subsequently turned into legislation – was reached in February 1996 on the (admittedly very limited) subject of part-time work for elderly workers (these part-time contracts being subsidized by the State if they are associated with new recruitments); second, a Pact for Employment was concluded in June 1996 for the Land of Bavaria and – what is more important – in April 1997 for the former Länder of the German Democratic Republic. Moreover, the philosophy underpinning the attempts to reach a country-wide agreement – basically the trade-off between wage moderation and job creation – has substantially inspired some branch agreements, such as those concluded in 1997 in the chemical industry.

As the focus so far has been on trends in central- and enterprise-level bargaining, we now examine the trends in sectoral collective bargaining, at the national or regional level. The available data show that it is still a very important component of many national industrial relations systems in the European countries discussed in this section. Indeed, the changes that have taken place over the past decade have not led to a major decline in sectoral collective bargaining, let alone its disappearance; rather, sectoral agreements are less precise than before and are now mainly designed to establish a broad framework for enterprise bargaining, leaving more room for manoeuvre to enterprise bargainers than was the case in the past.

In some countries, such as Italy and Belgium, the role of sectoral collective bargaining has even been reinforced in the recent past. The central agreement of July 1993 in Italy established a sophisticated system of "articulated bargaining", specifying how the subjects of bargaining would be distributed among the various levels of bargaining, as explained in more detail in Chapter 5. The framework laws promulgated in Belgium in 1996 after the failure of central negotiations have also introduced an elaborate bargaining system, which resembles the Italian system in some respects. For example, the framework law on wages prescribes, until the year 2000, a system of articulated bargaining with precise timing at the central, sectoral and enterprise levels. According to this system, the minimum and maximum levels of wage increases are fixed every second year through central bargaining, it being understood that, in the event of the failure of this negotiation, the Government would fix these minima and maxima itself. The actual wage bargaining will then mainly take place at the sectoral level. The framework law on job creation makes provision for a similar system, except that if central negotiations fail, the Government is not obliged to impose a decision on the parties, but can decide in each particular instance whether this seems appropriate or not.

It is, however, in the flexibilization of the labour market that sectoral bargaining continues to play a particularly important role. In this area, the parties at the central level only prescribe certain basic protections setting limits to the flexibility which the parties at lower levels can introduce. In practice, to the extent that the initiatives and innovations in labour market flexibility originate in collective bargaining at all (rather than in legislation, individual bargaining or employers' initiatives), they originate mostly in sectoral bargaining. The role of enterprise collective bargaining, although significant, is more limited in Belgium than in other countries mentioned in this section, except in the very few sectors, such as the chemical industry, where the bulk of collective bargaining has traditionally taken place at the enterprise level. Most enterprises do not seem to be taking advantage of the possibilities of enterprise flexibility bargaining offered by legislation, or by central or sectoral collective agreements.

While there are undeniably strong pressures to push the decentralization process further, there are also pressures in the opposite direction. For one thing, trade unions remain relatively strong in many European countries, and they generally favour higher-level bargaining. Moreover, the employers, who are in principle in favour of enterprise bargaining, are not always very adamant on this point for the following reasons:

- employers' organizations often have more sympathy for sectoral bargaining since it represents a substantial part of their *raison d'être;*
- a number of individual employers still have some sympathy for the idea of restricting competition and enhancing solidarity, which are at the basis of sectoral bargaining and which have a long tradition in Western Europe;
- many small and medium-sized enterprises prefer not to bargain themselves and would rather leave this task, for which they feel they are not really equipped, to employers' organizations; and
- certain big enterprises with strong unions sometimes prefer sectoral bargaining because sectoral agreements may be less costly for them than the agreements they would be able to negotiate at the enterprise level with their own unions.

Nevertheless, further pressure towards decentralization is very high, as is well illustrated by recent developments in Germany. In that country, which has a long tradition of sectoral bargaining, some employers, particularly in the metal industry, have recently begun to question the desirability of continuing this practice. Their main argument was that sectoral bargaining was no longer able to ensure the flexibility needed by enterprises to remain competitive. However, although the significance of this reappraisal of sectoral bargaining – as evidenced by an increasing inclusion of opening clauses in sectoral agreements – should certainly not be underestimated, it would be premature to conclude, as some already have done, that the German system of industrial relations, which has always been considered as one of the most solid bastions of the "European model" of sectoral bargaining, is on its way out. In fact, while there have been heated debates over the continued desirability of sectoral collective bargaining among employers in the metal industry, the employers' association of the chemical industry has recently published a position paper supporting sectoral bargaining.

Another illustration of the tensions existing with regard to the level of bargaining can be found in Belgium. The Global Plan of 1993 provided that (optional) employment promotion measures should be implemented through enterprise-level collective bargaining. However, the two bipartite central agreements which were concluded parallel to the Plan, for 1993–94 and 1995–96 respectively, provided for similar employment promotion measures to be negotiated at the sectoral level. This shows that – contrary to the Government – the central trade unions and the central employers' organizations preferred the sectoral level to the enterprise level and have actually transferred collective bargaining from the latter to the former (as far as employment-promotion measures are concerned).

The role of the State and the bargaining structure in Central and Latin America

The most drastic changes towards greater flexibility in the labour market have been introduced by several Latin American countries in the past decade. As mentioned earlier, most of these changes have been introduced unilaterally by governments through modifying legislation. Only Argentina has experienced the development of what one could call "collectively negotiated flexibilization", with the promulgation of the National Employment Act 1991. This Act created various types of flexible employment contracts, as in other countries, but – and this is new in the Latin American tradition of labour law – it also provided that the introduction of many of these types should be approved by sectoral collective agreements, and that the enterprises entering into flexible employment contracts should give copies of the contracts to the relevant trade unions. Moreover, both the Employment Act and the Small and Medium Enterprise Law 1995 have authorized collective agreements to establish the methods for calculating working days on the basis of monthly, six-monthly or annual averages.

The Government of Argentina has also played an increasing role as a party to industrial relations, as a result of its growing recognition of the autonomy of the social partners in this domain. Thus, it entered into a national tripartite agreement, the Framework Agreement for Employment, Competitiveness and Social Equity *(El Acuerdo Marco para el Empleo, la Competitividad y la Equidad Social)* on 25 July 1994 with the General Confederation of Labour (CGT) and central employers' organizations. The signatories of the Agreement have conceded that collective bargaining is the most appropriate procedure for introducing flexibility, and have introduced the concept of "agreed legislation" *(la legislación acordada)*, where the parties themselves define the issues and the content of the new legislation. However, the process of involving the social partners in regulating the labour market and industrial relations has not been a smooth one. For instance, in 1996, the Government sought to introduce various measures for enhancing labour market flexibility through legislation, without prior tripartite consultation. It nevertheless returned to the bargaining table in 1997 – but only with the CGT – to conclude a bilateral agreement on 9 May, reaffirming the parties' support for collective bargaining as a means of dealing with certain flexibility issues, including procedures for the termination of employment, and the residual effects of collective agreements after their expiry (an important issue in Argentina, where unions tend to rely on old collective agreements from 1975, instead of negotiating new flexibility agreements, given the stronger bargaining power of employers).

In other Latin American countries, as the State has continued to adopt highly interventionist policies towards collective labour relations, tripartite consultations and negotiations remain very ineffective when they are practised. This is typically the case in Peru, where social dialogue has not contributed to flexibility issues, and the failure of social dialogue over difficult economic and employment problems has forced the debate back into the legislative forum.

Not all Central and Latin American countries are beset by weak social dialogue, however. For example, tripartite consultations in Barbados have exerted a relatively strong influence over social agendas for many years. As a result, labour market flexibility has largely been introduced through tripartite consultations, although the Government has not manifested its formal position on the labour market flexibility issue. Noteworthy developments include the Protocol for the Implementation of a Prices and Incomes Policy, signed by representatives of the three social partners in 1993, followed by a second Protocol of 1995–97, and an addendum for the same biennium. In 1993, while discussions were under way with unions and associations in the public sector, the Government proposed an incomes policy calling for a wage freeze in both the public and private sectors, with exceptions to be made for increases due to productivity, and profit sharing. Out of this came the first Protocol, effective from April 1993 to March 1995. As a consequence, interest in productivity and profit sharing was heightened. Also during this period, the National Productivity Board became fully operational, giving advice on productivity techniques, and conducting training seminars on productivity, and the constraints to improving it. The Government has also encouraged bipartite negotiations over flexibility and rationalization in the port industry by giving assurances to port workers that they will pursue ways other than job cuts – presumably, training and retraining – to achieve the desired goals of rationalization. Encouraged by the Port Authority's assurances, the Barbados Workers Union is expected to take a more favourable stance on flexibility issues than would otherwise be the case (Blackman, 1997, p. 17).

In Latin American countries, collective bargaining takes place primarily at the enterprise level (with the exception of Argentina, Brazil, and Uruguay), even if the law allows bargaining at a higher level. However, unions have been trying to develop and implement sectoral-level collective bargaining, considered the preferred means for addressing broader labour market issues such as protection of atypical workers – which cannot be properly handled through enterprise-level bargaining. On the other hand, employers' organizations prefer to maintain collective bargaining at the enterprise level. In general, decentralized enterprise bargaining is the norm in most Latin American countries. Even countries such as Argentina and Brazil, which have held higher-level negotiations in the past, have begun to display a tendency towards decentralization.

The role of the State and the bargaining structure in Asia

In Asia, where trade unions have been relatively weak, collective bargaining has played a smaller role in the labour market, particularly in comparison with European countries. In most Asian countries, including Japan, the Republic of Korea and the Philippines, collective bargaining takes place primarily at the enterprise level. In India, however, higher-level agreements are more the norm, particularly in the public sector, and in the traditional jute and textile, and engineering industries. But even in India there has been a growing shift towards decentralized bargaining in the private sector, which will eventually reduce the role of employer-industry associations and central trade union organizations in collective bargaining. Such a development is already under way in the engineering and cement industries, and is expected to occur in the banking industry, which is already exposed to limited competition from private and multinational banks.

None the less, enterprise unionism and enterprise collective bargaining are the norm in other Asian countries, notably in Japan and the Republic of Korea. According to a 1990 survey in the Republic of Korea, for example, 98.1 per cent of unions were either enterprise or plant unions, while 72.2 per cent of all collective bargaining took place either at the enterprise or the plant level (Park and Park, 1991). In the Philippines, industry-level agreements exist in a few industries such as garments, but their content is very abstract, with the details fixed at the enterprise level.

The predominance of enterprise-level bargaining in Asia does not mean the absence of negotiations at the higher level, however. In fact, the annual wage negotiation round in Japan (*Shunto*) demonstrates a highly coordinated collective bargaining process at the industrial and national levels between enterprise unions and employers. In some sectors, Japanese enterprise unions have been successful in bringing employers to the industry-wide negotiations or bargaining table. A good example is an industry-level discussion forum (*sanbetsu roshi kaigi*) in the electrical machinery sector, dating back to 1972, which meets three times weekly in the spring to discuss shorter working hours, overtime premium pay and wages. A similar case can be found in the motor industry, where an industry-level Labour-Management Conference has been held since 1985 to discuss industrial restructuring and other labour-related issues. However, negotiations at the higher levels tend to be very informal, unlike the formal collective bargaining found in Western countries. The informality of industry-level negotiations tends to benefit employers because they can take advantage of one element of multi-employer bargaining (the placing of a floor under wage competition), without confronting the strong national or industrial unions (Sako, 1997). The existence of supra-enterprise institutional arrangements to coordinate the actions of individual enterprise unions and employers has enabled firms and unions to reach wage settlements that respond flexibly to changes in domestic and external pressures.

While collective bargaining in the Republic of Korea generally occurs at the enterprise level, there have been recent developments towards tripartite negotiations at the national level. For instance, the 1996–97 national tripartite negotiations over labour law reform, which were originally intended to enhance labour market flexibility while improving collective labour rights, made meaningful progress towards achieving social dialogue among the social partners in a country where authoritarian labour relations have dominated for more than three decades. The election of the new Government in December 1997 and the continuing economic crisis are likely to encourage further developments in tripartite social dialogue at the national level. Indeed, in February 1998, the social partners reached a "historic compromise" to introduce a lay-off system in return for the reform of *Chaebols* (Korean conglomerates), the strengthening of the social safety net – including the unemployment insurance fund – and significant improvements in freedom of association, including the legalization of teachers' rights to join trade unions and engage in collective bargaining. This national negotiation was carried out through a newly launched tripartite committee, composed of labour and finance ministers, representatives from the two national union centres, employers' associations, and *Chaebols*.

While the enterprise is certain to remain the primary level for collective bargaining, these new experiments in national tripartite negotiation will add a new dimension to the Korean industrial relations system. In fact, inadequacy of the social safety net and preponderance of corporate welfare provisions – especially among large firms – and the absence of higher-level bargaining have tended to overburden the agenda of enterprise bargaining, leaving little room for employers and unions to use collective bargaining at the enterprise level as a forum for dealing with a more productivity-oriented, mutual-gains agenda.

Concerning the role of the State, the Japanese Government has sometimes been interventionist, as exemplified in its legislative action, whether in connection with reducing hours of work after 1987, or reforming the pension system in 1986 and 1996. It also intervenes through measures to promote, for instance, the implementation of employment policy benefiting industries, regions, or categories of workers which have been placed in jeopardy by restructuring (ILO, 1997, p. 133). Furthermore, the Government has recently adopted a series of labour market deregulation policies, including a shift from the government placement monopoly system to one where public and private employment services co-exist, and legalization of the temporary work business. Discussions are also under way to extend the contract limitation period from one year to three or five years. Since the unemployment rate in Japan was still around 3 per cent in the mid-1990s, the emphasis of labour market deregulation is not on measures to counter unemployment, but rather on activating the external labour market. The Government thereby expects to attain a smooth reallocation of the workforce from declining to developing industries – without creating unemployment or disrupting workers' mobility (Araki, 1997).

The State also participates, although informally, in the national coordination process of annual wage bargaining. Rather than exhibiting direct control, it becomes indirectly involved in the tripartite interactions at the time of *Shunto*. Generally, the Government supports the wage increase recommendations made by such organizations as the Economic Planning Agency and the relevant ministries. Prior to *Shunto*, the rich network of bilateral and trilateral information exchange involving the Government enabled the social partners to implicitly arrive at the "rational" level of wage increases.

The role of the State in the Republic of Korea has undergone important changes in recent years. The advent of an independent union movement over the past decade has forced the State's role to change from one of repressive interventionist to active participant in industrial relations. Given the State's traditionally active role, particularly in the process of industrialization, it is almost certain that it will continue to play an important role in both the labour market and industrial relations. However, the Government is likely to put greater emphasis on creating a social safety in order to sustain a more flexible labour market, as well as support more autonomous industrial relations, whenever necessary, through active participation in tripartite social dialogue.

In India, where the tradition of pluralism has long existed, the Government has not taken any decisive measures to enhance labour market flexibility – largely because of its concern over the negative consequences of unbridled flexibility, not to mention concerns over union opposition to these changes. While there have been several attempts to introduce labour market flexibility, huge differences within and among the social partners have caused recent attempts at labour law reform to fail. However, it should also be noted that some state governments have already adopted employer-friendly policies, including promising a strike-free environment for five years from the date of investment, simplifying or centralizing inspections, cancelling registrations from unions which did not submit returns, and mandating secret ballots for union recognition. In addition, the judiciary has recently come out heavily against labour in the organized sector. Nevertheless, in matters concerning unprotected workers, including unorganized, contract and casual labour, the judiciary seems to be more protective of their plight (India country study).

While Indian labour laws appear to restrict employers' flexibility, in reality legal provisions are not as constraining as they appear on paper since law enforcement has been lax, particularly in areas such as minimum wages. This kind of discrepancy between the law and its enforcement has provided room for the Government to deliver a certain degree of unauthorized flexibility, even without significant legislative changes which might entail social conflict.

The situation is more or less the same in the Philippines. For instance, while some forms of labour flexibility come under the category of labour-only contracting, which is prohibited by law, the Government tolerates such practices because of the alleged triple benefits of: (i) allowing companies to be more globally competitive; (ii) encouraging expansion, and therefore creating new employment opportunities; and (iii) helping develop new entrepreneurs or providing assistance to small entrepreneurs in terms of technology, markets and overall improved capability. A 1990 survey by the Institute of Labor Studies of the Philippines revealed that labour laws had virtually no influence (1.3 per cent) on an employer's decision on whether or not to hire contract labour. It implies that even without significant legislative initiatives, governments in developing countries can introduce a certain degree of labour market flexibility through loose enforcement of the legislation.

Concluding remarks

No doubt, the decline in union density and decentralization of collective bargaining are posing great challenges to the existing systems of industrial relations in many countries, and have even led to a shrinking influence of collective bargaining. Nevertheless, as the experiences of these selected countries reveal, collective industrial relations continue to play an important role in addressing both labour market flexibilization and the interests of working people. While the focus of collective bargaining has moved towards the enterprise level, it is clear that tripartite and bipartite negotiations at the higher levels have been instrumental in enhancing labour market flexibility and addressing broader social agendas. The role of the State also remains critical in many countries, particularly given the volatility of markets and the persistence of high unemployment rates. Thus, how to achieve an optimal balance between the State and market demand, as well as among different levels of collective bargaining, will continue to be a focal point of debate for all social partners in the world.

THE POSITIONS OF THE SOCIAL PARTNERS ON LABOUR MARKET FLEXIBILITY

4

Introduction

As discussed earlier, the role of the State and the structure of collective bargaining have had to adapt themselves to changing labour market conditions. So, too, have the social partners, as competitive pressures, increasingly global markets and rapid technological changes have caused trade unions and employers to rethink their policies and positions. The issue of flexibility has sparked a diversity of opinions between, and even among, the social partners.

Employers have been the driving force, and advocates for, labour market flexibility in most countries from the beginning of the push towards flexibilization. However, there has been substantial variation in the way in which they pursue labour market flexibility. Evidence also suggests that there is a discrepancy between employers' ideological enthusiasm for labour market flexibility and their practical adoption of flexibility measures. On the side of trade unions, too, there exists the same diversity across countries, sectors and occupations. While trade unions in most countries initially took a defensive and reactive position opposing flexibility, the mounting pressure towards labour market flexibility forced many of them to reconsider their traditional approaches and to adopt a more sustainable strategy towards labour market flexibility by the first half of the 1990s. Declining union density, ever-increasing unemployment and a growing number of atypical workers have been the primary factors forcing unions to reconsider their strategies and policies. Thus, as evidence from 22 countries shows, the social partners today seem to share the common notion that labour market flexibility should be enhanced to cope with global competition and to create better jobs.

Nevertheless, the shared notion of the need to enhance labour market flexibility does not necessarily guarantee a shared approach among the social partners. Even though labour market flexibilization may have the potential to stimulate economic growth and create more jobs, it also poses a challenge to maintaining sufficient protection for vulnerable populations – a matter previously addressed by either existing labour legislation or the collective industrial relations system. It is therefore understandable that the social partners have different and, in many cases opposing, views and approaches to flexibility issues. In particular, unilateral decisions regarding labour market flexibility and infringement of collective labour rights in pursuing it may lead to social unrest, as shown in a recent general strike in the Republic of Korea.

The countries in this study have taken diverse approaches towards labour market flexibility because of the different historical, institutional and economic contexts in which the social partners are placed. The same is true of the role of collective bargaining in labour market flexibility. Different views and policies are observed not only among the social partners in different countries, but also within the same party in the same country; approaches may vary according to sector, occupation, level of the organization (enterprise, industry or national level), size of firm and so on.

Employers' positions

For the most part, employers have been the primary advocates for labour market flexibility and deregulation. Faced with growing competition among countries, as well as among enterprises, they are increasingly calling for flexible work arrangements. As expressed by the Irish Business and Employers Confederation (IBEC), employers think that flexibility is "essential to equip enterprises to compete in this ever diminishing globe" and that maximum flexibility in work practices is needed to organize production and services to respond to rapidly changing markets (Ireland country study). Chronic unemployment, combined with the growing locational freedom of enterprises due to economic globalization, has given employers a stronger bargaining position in many countries.

Against this backdrop, employers around the world have been largely success-ful in putting forward their flexibilization agenda. Emphasizing the principle of freedom of contracts, employers and their organizations have expressed the opinion that only in the case of an unacceptable use of flexible work relations should legal measures be taken. In many countries, they began to complain openly about "rigid" labour markets and "rigid" labour legislation, which employers view as major obstacles to labour market flexibility.

Concerning collective bargaining, employers across the countries studied have shown a clear preference towards rule making at a decentralized level (i.e. the enterprise or plant level), as well as a preference for the active involvement of works councils rather than trade unions. Increasingly, they have begun to distance them-selves from centralized bargaining, favouring decentralized enterprise bargaining.

At the extreme, employers' organizations in some countries, such as New Zealand, have shown their preference for individual contract arrangements instead of collective agreements.

However, employers have by no means had free reign. They have had to operate within the web of legislative regulations and the different institutional contexts of labour-management relations. In particular, as far as labour issues are concerned, there have been two opposing currents of opinion among employers and their representative organizations across the world. For example, employers in the United States, and to a lesser degree those in Canada, clearly favour the freedom to manage industrial relations within their own organizations. Under these circumstances, employers' organizations have had little room to play an active role in labour-management relations and labour market issues. A second point of view, which is popular in European countries, favours regulating conditions of employment, and even other conditions of production, at higher levels. The objective here is to avoid uncontrolled competition, which may be to everyone's disadvantage, and ensure stability (ILO, 1997, p. 62). In many developing countries, employers' organizations are not influential, mainly because of the difficulty in coordinating the actions of the various sectors of the economy and in uniting diverging interests. Thus in India, divisions among employers' organizations tend to hinder employers from having one voice on labour market flexibility issues.

Aside from the different national contexts in which employers and their organizations are placed, in many cases, the sector and size of firms have also made a difference to how employers approach flexibility. More importantly, an individual employer's approach may be different from that of an employers' organization, as is also the case with trade unions. None the less, as individual employers normally adopt pragmatic attitudes towards flexibility, we cannot talk of any clear-cut models of flexible firms, as described by some researchers.

However, one cannot deny that the intensifying competition in both global and domestic markets has increased the pressure on employers to pursue more aggressive strategies towards flexible management of human resources and to redefine labour-management relations. As in Australia, New Zealand and some European countries such as Germany and Sweden, this pressure tends to encourage a shift in the role of employers' organizations, which have been pillars of the traditional industrial relations system in these countries.

It is clear that employers generally want to introduce labour market flexibility by exercising their managerial rights without being subject to any restrictions resulting from legislation or trade union action. However, their search for the full extent of flexibility may have inherent limits arising from general conditions of competition and employer-employee relationships, even without legislative and collective intrusion into management. In this section, we highlight the intrinsic limits placed on employers' policies of enterprise flexibility, as well as the rationale for such flexibility.

Employment flexibility

Employers and their organizations are strong advocates of employment flexibility, as they regard rigid regulation of employment contracts as an obstacle to their efforts to adapt to changing market situations. Therefore, they are increasingly calling for the removal of regulatory provisions over their power to hire and fire, such as relaxing the restrictions on recourse to flexible forms of employment, including temporary agency work, part-time work and fixed-term work. As described in Chapter 1, casual and other forms of non-standard employment have been increasing throughout the world.

Whether the casualization of the workforce and the proliferation of non-standard employment are the result of employers' "flexible firm" strategies remains unclear (Atkinson, 1984). For instance, survey evidence in Australia suggests that employers' recourse to casual and other forms of non-standard labour was largely a reflection of labour market and product market factors, rather than the general adoption of a "flexible firm" strategy by employers. The available evidence suggests that the increase in non-standard employment is primarily associated with cost-minimization strategies as Australian employers react to recessions and increased competition (Brosnan and Thornwaite, 1994, cited in the Australia country study).

Employers are also aware of the possible drawbacks of flexible employment. Indeed, although they may generally be in favour of expanding flexible employment as a means of becoming more responsive to increasingly volatile market conditions, many of them also see the disadvantages associated with the use of casual employment. For instance, Australian employers, particularly those in firms with a complex labour process or where expensive machinery is operated, refer to the drawbacks associated with the casualization of the workforce, such as lack of commitment to the firm and the extra administrative burden (Brosnan, 1996, pp. 30–35, cited in the Australia country study). Philippines' employers in the electronics industry appear to employ fewer non-regular workers than those in the garment industry, because their comparatively more complex production processes require a greater input of skilled labour and more quality control (the Philippines country study). The same reasoning led Ford Motor Company in the United States to limit the size of its contingent workforce. At present, contingent workers comprise no more than 10 to 15 per cent of the total. Ford found it impractical to use contingent workers in certain situations, especially in core operations that demand a flexible, well-trained workforce. Companies such as Ford are discovering that contingent workers may save money in the short run, but their lack of skills and experience can prove costly over the long run (Burkins, 1996, cited in the United States country study).

Wage flexibility

Employers have generally exhibited a preference for various flexible compensation schemes over rigid wage structures such as seniority-based systems, which they believe lack elements to encourage higher productivity and performance by employees. They prefer flexible payments for two primary reasons: first, they allow employers to adjust the total wage bill to the business cycle; second, they motivate employees to enhance their performance and productivity by creating a direct link with pay. In their view, for example, gain sharing can help motivate workers and focus their energy, improve productivity, and link pay to business results. Quite often, employees' participation schemes, which aim to draw workers into the decision-making process of the organization (albeit more frequently at the shop-floor than at the corporate level), incorporate gain-sharing plans. Employers generally believe that such plans help workers make the connection between specific factors that need to be improved, such as customer service or quality, and the overall competitiveness of the company.

However, flexible compensation schemes are not without their problems, even for employers. In the Netherlands, for example, the majority of companies in a recent survey have indicated that in practice it is difficult to determine the objectives to be achieved and to actually apply the variable pay scheme, in particular if the results turn out to be below the "target" level (Hay Consultants, 1996, cited in the Netherlands country study). Despite a widespread aspiration among employers for greater individualization of pay rates and bonuses through some form of merit- or competency-based system, there was wide recognition that the key problem was "how to operate a successful differential pay scheme". Problems of finding suitable and acceptable measurement criteria were referred to, and one respondent reported the withdrawal of an appraisal-related pay scheme because employees perceived it to be unfair. Some employers in the United Kingdom realized that the alteration of job grades had to be related to the introduction of "single status" terms and conditions and a move away from an hourly to a salaried basis for pay (United Kingdom country study).

In countries with a tradition of centralized industrial relations, such as Norway, Sweden and now Ireland, employers' attitudes towards flexibility and the decentralization of the bargaining process have been rather ambivalent, in the sense that they are very much concerned about preventing the escalation of wage increases; this is due to the strong union presence in the workplace, combined with relatively low unemployment in the local labour market. The employers' dilemma in wage policy lies in the need to coordinate the bargaining process at the central level in order to secure wage moderation, while enhancing flexibility at the company level (Ibsen, 1997, p. 180). However, the increasing competition in both domestic and global markets has driven employers to pursue decentralized wage determination in order to gain wage flexibility. In particular, multinational companies tend to be more aggressive in pursuing decentralized wage bargaining while departing from centralized bargaining, as was quite evident in the Swedish engineering industries.

Countries with a tradition of decentralized collective bargaining tend to have difficulties in enhancing macro-level wage flexibility, especially in ensuring wage moderation in the face of escalating competition. The failure of a "social accord" at the national level in the Republic of Korea illustrates this point. Concerned about the declining competitiveness of Korean industries due to rapidly rising wage levels, the Korean Employers Federation signed two consecutive national bipartite (1993) and tripartite (1994) agreements on wage increases with the Federation of Korean Trade Unions (FKTU), supported by the Government. Employers wished to moderate wage increases in exchange for some improvements in social protection provisions such as unemployment insurance schemes. Yet a number of factors, including the lack of consensus among workers, union rivalry, and the lack of organizational leverage on the part of both employers and trade unions – due to the highly segmented enterprise bargaining system – made it difficult to translate these national agreements into practice at the enterprise level. On the other hand, despite difficulties in coordinating action at higher levels among both employers and unions – also due to the enterprise bargaining system – employers in Japan have been able to achieve macroeconomic wage flexibility through highly elaborated, but informal coordination among employers in the export sector. In this case, micro-level cooperation between unions and management at the enterprise level has facilitated informal coordination between them, and among employers at higher levels.

Working-time flexibility

In order to meet fluctuating market demands, companies have been seeking to make working-time arrangements more flexible. Such arrangements may also be introduced as part of wider restructuring in response to external threats to the enterprise, and may be associated with certain compensatory factors relating to reduced working time, and new pay and leave entitlements.

In countries such as the Netherlands and Germany, employers' search for greater working-time flexibility was prompted by unions' demands for shorter working hours as a mean of creating jobs. While not opposing the unions' demands for collective working-time reductions, Dutch employers instead proposed more flexible arrangements; for example, the total number of annual working hours should be stipulated in collective agreements and each enterprise should be left to negotiate detailed arrangements with the trade unions. The proposal was agreed to by the unions subject to certain conditions (such as setting limits on the number of daily working hours). The destandardization of contracts and the new hours regime added fuel to the continuing process of decentralization of Dutch industrial relations. Furthermore, the 35-hour week, which the German unions wanted to establish collectively as a new employment standard for all employees, triggered employers' search for flexibilizing and decentralizing the collective bargaining system. Likewise, the Confederation of Norwegian Business and Industry (NHO) has proposed that issues related to working time should be dealt with through local agreements with significant scope for individual variation, rather than through law or industry-wide collective agreements, as is now the case. Moreover, the introduction of a variety of flexible leave provisions in Norway, such as parental leave and educational leave, has further prompted employers to look for other means of making the labour supply more flexible, including more liberal regulations on the use of temporary employment and private temporary help agencies.

Despite their general interest in greater flexibility in working-time arrangements, employers in some countries have failed to exploit the full range of options. For instance, only 9 per cent of all employees in the United Kingdom were working under annualized working hours schemes in 1993 (Watson, 1994, cited in the United Kingdom country study). Of course, annualized working time gives employers various benefits: a reduction in overtime and temporary employment costs; greater operational flexibility, facilitating continuous production and the adjustment of labour input to changing requirements; improved productivity and reduced absenteeism; and the opportunity to introduce multi-skilling and task flexibility on the job (IRS, 1991, ibid.). The scheme also entails certain disadvantages, such as the complexity of scheduling holidays and shift rotas, and employees' resistance to unrostered hours. Workers might also experience difficulties in planning leisure and family time if they are frequently on call at short notice or if they have to work long hours for certain periods. As annualization of working time affects such crucial issues as basic salaries, overtime and shift premiums, as well as the conditions for utilizing reserve hours, it often involves tough negotiations. The complexity of annualized hours systems, and the potential resistance of employees, might help explain their relatively limited application.

Work organization and skill formation

One notable trend in employers' policies on work organization over the past decade has been a growing recognition of the crucial link between work organization and competitiveness. As discussed in Chapter 1, pressure for changes in the organization of work has emanated from a number of related sources: intensified competition; new technology requiring multi-skilling and enabling new work organization in practice; new work concepts such as just in time (JIT), total quality management (TQM) and total productive maintenance (TPM); and changes in external labour markets encouraging employers to take more systematic steps to develop and retain the skills of their key employees. It is in this context that employers have sought organizational reforms which enable them to gain more benefit from employees' work-related knowledge and skills, and to integrate quality control into production processes. To bring about changes in work organization, employers are increasingly eager to involve employees and/or unions in the process of continuous quality and productivity improvement, as well as promote teamwork.

However, in spite of the common pressures on employers to pursue work organization flexibility, employers' organizations and individual employers have pursued a wide range of approaches to this matter. As one author put it –

employers' policies on work organization are more coherently formulated in countries where employers' organizations play a relatively important role in the coordination of employers' labour relations policies (e.g. Germany and Japan), than in those where such organizations traditionally play a minor role (as in the United States) or where their importance has recently been declining (as in the United Kingdom). In the latter countries, employers' policies on work organization (as on other issues) have to be inferred from the behaviour of many individual enterprises (Ozaki, 1996a, p. 39).

Japanese employers, most notably those in the motor industry, have been the front-runners in innovative work organization, developing the new system of lean production which enables flexible deployment of employees through multi-skilling and allows rapid adjustments to ever-changing market demands. This flexible work organization has been supported by employers' greater emphasis on the importance of continuous on-the-job training as a key element in developing and maintaining Japan's competitive edge. Thus companies have consistently increased the amount and levels of training within the enterprise. Since the oil crisis of the early 1970s, Japanese industry has sought to raise quality while containing costs by using more flexible systems of production and procurement, based on microelectronic and JIT delivery techniques. The presence of the Japanese Productivity Centre, which is basically a tripartite body, contributed to the spread of these innovative practices throughout entire industries in Japan.

In countries such as the United Kingdom and the United States, where trade unions tend to exert a great deal of influence over detailed job content in an attempt to defend their members' interests, employers have had difficulties in introducing new work organization which might undermine existing job demarcations, and hence unions' leverage to control the workplace. Recently, however, evolving technology and changing determinants of enterprise competitiveness have driven employers in these countries to introduce new ways of organizing work, blurring traditional distinctions between the work of particular crafts. In a more recent study, referred to in Chapter 1, the New Zealand Institute for Economic Research reported that reduced occupational demarcations and greater multi-skilling were two of the substantial changes that managers have perceived since 1991 (NZIER, 1996, p. 9). In countries with a tradition of job-control unionism, as well as in newly industrializing and developing countries such as the Republic of Korea and India, employers are generally reluctant to associate unions with questions of work organization. For instance, employers in the Republic of Korea often try to use empowerment of foremen and workers as an instrument for undermining union influence, as well as for enhancing competitiveness. A large majority of employers in the United States also regard unions as a hindrance to productivity and are unwilling to recognize them, let alone allow them to participate in decision-making on work organization. However, it is also true that labour-management innovation in the United States is characterized by an impressive degree of union participation in management at the local level. The less well-developed institutional and regulatory framework of industrial relations in the United States sometimes provides scope for innovations and flexible adaptation to changing environments by individual firms. Some American companies, such as Xerox and General Motors' Saturn, have been able to develop fundamentally new ways of organizing employment relationships and new production systems when employers and unions have agreed to the creation of new forums for labour-management consultation.

By contrast, employers in Italy and Sweden are relatively favourable to union participation in work organization. In Italy, where the unions were very active in the 1980s promoting group-based work organization, "employers widely regard collective bargaining as the main means of organizing work and promoting direct participation of workers" (Ozaki, 1996a, p. 41). Like their counterparts elsewhere, however, Italian employers favoured weaker forms of employee involvement such as quality circles rather than group-based autonomous work organization, which the unions tend to prefer (Lansbury, Kochan and MacDuffie, 1997, p. 9). In general, Swedish employers "accept the principle of union/ management cooperation in developing work organization, as illustrated by the 1982 Efficiency and

Participation Agreement between the central organizations of employers and workers in the private sector, which was concluded under the Co-determination at Work Act of 1976" (Ozaki, 1996a, p. 41).

While admitting the benefits of employees' involvement in work organization, employers generally consider that unions' involvement slows down the decision-making process which is crucial for timely adaptation. For this reason, some Swedish employers have been reluctant to allow more union participation. Also, the metal industry employers' organization in Germany is strongly opposed both to the introduction of organizational changes through collective bargaining and to the extension of works councils' co-determination rights to work organization issues (Jacobi and Hassel, 1996, pp.111–113, ibid., p. 40). However, at the enterprise level – at least in larger firms – management generally seems to believe that rationalization projects cannot circumvent the works council, because the success of such projects largely depends on their acceptance by, and motivation of, employees.

There also appears to have been a greater standardization of work in some industrial sectors (certain occupations in telecommunications, services and banking), and a greater diversification in others (steel, motor vehicles, airlines). In the latter areas, there are more flexible job definitions and fewer demarcations, as well as greater multi-skilling, use of teamwork, networks and a fusion of task planning and execution. These innovations are found primarily in firms and industries which are engaged in international competition, have embraced technological and other changes, and have involved their employees and/or unions in decision-making. Yet such firms and industries tend to be in the minority.

In Norway and Sweden, the development of new forms of work organization has driven employers to question the traditional division between blue-collar and white-collar workers. A new proposal challenging this division, put forward by the NHO, proposes to replace current agreements with local vertical agreements covering all employees in one enterprise. In the same vein, the Swedish Employers' Confederation (SAF) has also been advancing a so-called "co-worker" agreement since 1987. The overall idea is to provide equal terms of employment for all employees in a company, where everyone shares the same wage system but may be members of different trade unions. This innovation is the result of two processes: one involves the growing inability of the centralized model to manage the wage-fixing process; the other – which is more important – has to do with changes in work organization. Over the past decade, work organization in many Swedish industries shifted from the old Taylorist style to a type of organization emphasizing integration, flexibility and participation. As a result, the demarcation between blue- and white-collar workers has been blurred. Thus, the co-worker agreement seems to result from the need to integrate blue- and white-collar work, as well as the need for a more decentralized wage structure in order to support flexibility and a more efficient work organization.

Trade unions' positions

Trade unions around the world have been struggling to cope with the wave of labour market flexibilization over the last decade, in an era of steady decline in union density and weakening bargaining power of trade unions. For some time after labour market flexibility became a topical issue in labour relations, trade unions generally took a defensive and reactive stance on the subject. The depth and breadth of the drive towards labour market flexibility during the last decade, however, drove many trade unions to reconsider and reformulate their policies on the matter. While unions in many countries today regard labour market flexibility as an inevitable means of coping with the deteriorating labour market situation (i.e. the persistence of high unemployment rates), they are confronted with the task of reconciling their traditional strategy and function with new approaches to labour market flexibility.

As union membership in most countries has largely been confined, until recently, to full-time employees with an employment contract of unspecified duration, the spread of flexible employment has posed a number of very serious challenges to trade unions. For example, unions now have to organize and protect a growing number of workers under atypical employment contracts, who are often placed under unfavourable employment conditions or even excluded from the scope of application of protective labour legislation. Moreover, they have to reconcile the interests of their traditional members with those of these contingent workers.

At the micro level also, trade unions in many countries are becoming keen on enhancing the competitiveness and productivity of enterprises, regarded as a prerequisite for preserving or creating jobs. The increasingly favourable attitude which many trade unions are now adopting towards work reforms within enterprises points to this changing policy. In so far as flexibility measures are introduced through negotiation or consultation with trade unions and are not intended to upset the balance of power between unions and management, unions tend to react positively to flexibilization. By their nature, of course, they are against measures unilaterally taken by employers which might result in the deterioration of their members' well-being.

The decentralization of collective bargaining is also compelling unions in some countries to adapt their structure and strategy to new environments, while in countries where union and bargaining structures have already been decentralized for many decades, pressures for structural change have generally been weaker. As a result of the diversity among trade union structures, strategic choices and institutional arrangements, unions' responses to labour market flexibility have varied widely from one country to another.

Employment flexibility

A primary concern of unions over the past decade has been their members' employment security. As a general strike in the Republic of Korea in early 1997 demonstrated, government attempts to ease restrictions on employers' freedom to dismiss workers have often met with strong union opposition. In particular, the hard stance of Korean trade unions on employment protection seems to have come from the inadequacy of the social safety net and a heavy reliance on corporate welfare provisions. The French national trade union organizations, the General Confederation of Labour (CGT) and *Force Ouvrière* (FO), are of the view that employment contracts should be signed on a permanent basis, with a recourse to fixed-term contracts only in exceptional cases. This is why the FO did not sign the national collective agreements of March 1990 which specified the rules of recourse to fixed-term contracts. When unions agree to accept employment adjustments to cope with economic difficulties, they often prefer other methods such as transfers within corporate groups (Japan, Republic of Korea), conversion into part-time contracts (for example, France, Italy), and even franchising contracts whereby employees faced with redundancy are offered the opportunity to open a shop selling the company's products (Telecom Italy).

Unions elsewhere have had difficulty in developing effective strategies to protect contingent workers, partly because such workers appear reluctant to embrace trade unionism. For instance, as the ACTU put it: "Part-time workers often regard employment and unionism as of marginal importance to their lives; and many casual workers change jobs frequently, disrupting any links with unions" (cited in Olney, 1996, p. 22). In countries where enterprise-level unions predominate, the unions themselves appear to make little effort to organize and protect contingent workers. According to one survey in the Republic of Korea, only 4.3 per cent of trade unions allow part-timers to join trade unions (Yoon, 1996).

Legal barriers can also frustrate trade unions' efforts to organize atypical workers. In the United States, for instance, the granting of exclusive union representation for particular bargaining units poses a distinct problem, since the workers in the bargaining unit should share a "community of interest", which may be absent between full-time and contingent workers (Olney, 1996, pp. 22–23). Indeed, contingent workers in the United States are far less likely to be unionized, or to work at jobs covered by a union contract, than non-contingent workers. In fact, roughly 9 per cent of contingent workers are covered by a union contract, compared to 17.5 per cent of non-contingent workers. Moreover, union density in the manufacturing and service sectors was only one-third as high among contingent workers as among non-contingent workers (United States country study). This situation has sometimes led American trade unions to adopt defensive strategies focused on minimizing the use of contingent workers. One such approach has consisted of limiting the percentage of part-timers among the total workforce, while another has required permanent status for temporary workers after the lapse of a specified period. The United Autoworkers (UAW), for example, has used the strategy of accepting the use of temporary workers, and then finding ways of moving them into permanent union jobs. Thus, American trade unions appear to focus on protecting regular workers' employment security, without making much effort to organize or protect contingent workers as such – although there is evidence from some unions (notably the Service Employees International Union (SEIU), the American Federation of State, County and Municipal Employees (AFSCME) and the United Food and Commercial Workers (UFCW)) that these practices may be changing.

In continental European countries, unions have tended to pursue somewhat different strategies for contingent workers, ranging from seeking to influence their compensation and working conditions to exploiting the advantages of contingent work for employees, or to pushing for public subsidies for contingent workers (Wever, 1997). For example, the German Confederation of Trade Unions (DGB), and the British Trades Union Congress (TUC) proposed to extend legislation and collective agreements to encompass contingent workers (Olney, 1996, p. 23).

In this respect, Dutch trade unions have taken the most proactive policy measures to provide due protection to this type of worker. They are very much in favour of improving the legal status of workers in flexible employment, and have advocated revising the law on employment contracts for this purpose. In addition, they have been advocating improvements in social security for flexible workers. They argue (as does the Swedish Trade Union Confederation, the LO) that flexible workers should have social security benefits comparable and equivalent to those of "normal" workers (the Netherlands country study). This policy of Dutch unions has achieved some success, as shown in the document published by the Minister of Social Affairs and Employment in December 1995, proposing the introduction of a certain degree of flexibility into the employment contracts of "permanent" workers, while strengthening protections for temporary workers. Dutch trade unions are also in favour of more flexibilization as long as decisions on the subject, and the ways they are to be implemented, are not left exclusively in the hands of the employer, but are part of the collective rule-making complex (through law, collective agreements, consultation with works councils and so on). However, the proactive approach that the unions have taken regarding contingent workers may largely reflect the voluntary nature of atypical employment in the Netherlands. Indeed, more than in other European countries, the growth of part-time and temporary employment in the country is mainly supply-side driven – largely stimulated by diminishing cultural impediments to, and prejudice against, such work. Generally, trade unions are favourably disposed to contingent employment of a voluntary nature, not only in the Netherlands but in other countries as well, as shown, for example, by the attitude of the French FO unions. On the other hand, unions tend to be quite critical of flexible employment of an involuntary nature.

Wage flexibility

The ability of trade unions to deliver macroeconomic wage flexibility, which benefits both employment and economic growth, largely depends on the collective bargaining structure (both horizontal and vertical) and its institutional context, while there are by no means linear relationships between the bargaining structure and economic performance (Traxler and Kittel, 1997). For example, highly centralized Norwegian trade unions appear to have been able to help bring about macroeconomic stability through moderate wage demands at the national level under the "solidarity alternative" policy in 1992. In Ireland, where collective bargaining has been recentralized since 1987 at the initiative of the Irish Congress of Trade Unions (ICTU), the macro-level wage policies have been instrumental in achieving economic growth through below-average annual wage increases. On the other hand, Japanese trade unions, which are mainly organized at the enterprise level, have been successful in delivering macro-level wage flexibility in spite of the highly decentralized system of bargaining. Since the oil crisis in the 1970s, enterprise unions in export sectors such as the motor, electronics, steel and shipbuilding industries have developed a highly elaborate system of coordinating wage demands among unions in the industries, while fully taking into account the macroeconomic situation and competitiveness of Japanese export industries. With corresponding informal coordination among employers in the export sector, this coordinated behaviour of Japanese enterprise unions has provided unions in other sectors with a bargaining pattern that is largely in line with macroeconomic indicators.

As pointed out in Chapter 1, there has been a proliferation over the past decade of contingent payment schemes linking wages to employees' performance and company profits. For example, the seniority-based pay structures of manual workers in organized sectors in the United States have been eroded by alternative compensation schemes which tie workers' wages to such factors as company profits or a work team's performance. And in Japan, the seniority-based wage structure, which has been regarded as one of the three pillars of the Japanese industrial relations system, is increasingly giving way to performance-related pay (PRP).

Unions' response to flexible wage schemes has been mixed. Some trade unions, like those in the Philippines, welcomed new work organization and new pay schemes, believing that the schemes would deliver wage increases. On the other hand, some Korean trade unions have opposed the introduction of PRP based on personnel appraisals, lest the schemes weaken solidarity among union members.

Some surveys appear to provide evidence that the presence of trade unions is not a facilitating factor in implementing individualized PRP schemes. For example, there is evidence showing that non-union organizations in Ireland are more likely to use individual PRP, group bonus schemes and profit sharing than unionized ones. In the case of merit payments, or PRP, the difference between union and non-union organizations is particularly significant at the clerical level. Although this form of incentive, which has traditionally been associated with managerial employees, is moving down the organizational hierarchy in non-union firms, it is not occurring to the same extent in unionized ones, particularly where manual employees are concerned (Ireland country study). In the Netherlands, too, flexible remuneration played a less significant role in the wage movements of workers covered by collective agreements than of those who were not.

While trade unions are generally critical of individual PRP, they seem to be more in favour of group-based performance pay, as is the case, for example, among Dutch unions. Likewise, the Swedish LO trade unions fear that individual PRP would introduce an element of arbitrariness into the wage-fixing process, and would therefore not allow such "individual setting of wage rates" unless the local trade unions were able to influence the decision making on ability and performance criteria. The same tendency was reported in Ireland, where a greater percentage of unionized than non-union organizations use group bonus schemes for manual employees. This may be a result of trade union opposition to individual pay schemes, favouring group rewards instead. But unions' policies on individual and group-based PRP may not be the same as individual employees' attitudes. For example, a recent survey among members of the Netherlands Trade Union Confederation (FNV) indicated that a majority of younger members (below age 30) support a remuneration system with more possibilities for individual differentiation linked to performance and education levels.

Unions are generally critical of the new wage schemes which might impinge upon their role in determining pay. Irish unions' willingness to accept group bonus schemes can be explained partly by the fact that these schemes do not work against the role of unions in formulating basic wages – they comprise only a bonus, not the base wage. Furthermore, they represent a group, rather than an individual reward, which minimizes the risk of favouritism. Unions are often more likely to support the use of variable pay schemes if they are over and above the base compensation. Thus, trade unions in the United States accept gain sharing when it is used as an extra bonus for rewarding higher productivity, but not as a basic part of the compensation package.

Besides a fear that flexible wage schemes might entail favouritism and a weakening of solidarity among union members, trade union federations like the American Federation of Labor and Congress of Industrial Organizations (AFL-CIO) in the United States have expressed concern about how much control workers have over the various elements that go into these new compensation schemes. For example, if the quality of products is a measure of performance, workers need to be able to control the factors that determine quality. In the same vein, Italian trade unions have highlighted the difficulty of evaluating the performance of individual organizational units without considering problems of efficiency and quality arising from the previous stages of the production process (Italy country study). Dutch trade unions have pointed out the difficulties of determining individual contributions to an organization's success, particularly at the lower levels, as a reason for opposing pay systems linked to individual performance (the Netherlands country study). Another misgiving unions have about gain-sharing schemes is that higher productivity rates could lead to workforce reductions. Accordingly, the United Autoworkers union (UAW) in the United States insisted during the 1995 bargaining rounds with the motor industry that productivity increases should not have negative effects on the jobs of current workers. A year into the agreement, however, the union found out that, although current workers were protected, the company had begun reducing the size of the workforce through attrition.

Working-time flexibility

Although the reduction of working time has always been a central concern of trade unions, working-time issues have now taken on new dimensions. Besides the traditional concern for working time reducing as a means of improving workers' living conditions, other concerns such as job creation, enterprise flexibility and striking a balance between work and family life have prompted trade unions around the world to develop new approaches to the issue. To cite one example of changing union policy towards working time, the FO in France, although critical of labour market flexibility in general, signed an agreement with the CNPF on 31 October 1995 on the flexibilization of working time, providing for – *inter alia* – annualization of working time. In return, the CNPF signed an agreement which introduced the reduction of working time in order to create employment. Other national union centres such as the Democratic Confederation of Labour (CFDT), the French

Confederation of Christian Workers (CFTC) and the French Confederation of Executive Staffs (CGC) have also accepted annualization of working time, but only in exchange for reducing working time without a reduction in wages. Working-time flexibility frequently raises questions of pay as well. In Norway, trade unions often regard employers' demands for the introduction of shift work or annualization of hours as a wage cut; Korean trade unions have opposed employers' flexible working hours schemes on the same grounds.

Other unions, including those in Germany and the Netherlands, have been drawn into debates on working-time flexibility after their demands for shorter hours provoked employers' to push for more flexible arrangements. This was the case, for example, with the campaign for the 35-hour week launched by German unions in the mid-1980s, which touched off the employers' strenuous search for more flexibility and differentiation of collective bargaining regulations (Germany country study). In the same vein, shorter working time in the Netherlands led to the introduction of non-standard contracts and hours of work. In Australia, increasing flexibility in the way that hours of work are arranged was one of the major reasons for introducing enterprise bargaining, as it allows for deviations from standardized working time that meet the specific needs of the enterprise. This is confirmed by the fact that 100 per cent of the agreements registered between January and July 1995 included provisions for greater flexibility in starting and finishing times and/or flexibility in setting hours of work (Australia country study).

Certain discrepancies are discernible between the policies pursued by the national trade union centres, which tend to place greater emphasis on reducing regular working hours and overtime, and the policies pursued by local unions or the aspirations of their rank-and-file members. For example, the LO in Norway has called for a reduction in overtime, but this has not necessarily been followed up by the local branches. The LO was aiming to create jobs by reducing overtime, while workers preferred to increase their earnings by working longer hours (Norway country study). Workers' keen interest in overtime as a means of increasing their earnings may be dissuading some unions from agreeing to flexible working-time arrangements such as annualized working hours. This was the case in the Republic of Korea, for example, where trade unions opposed the introduction of a flexible working-time scheme in 1996 expressly because they wished to maintain their overtime pay.

Work organization

In countries where trade unions have made an effort to control job content, as in Canada, the United Kingdom and the United States, they have tended to resist changes in work organization more strongly than their counterparts in other

105

countries. For example, collective agreements in the United States have traditionally had detailed provisions specifying job categories. As a result, any attempt by the enterprise to reorganize work has necessitated lengthy negotiations with the unions over changes in job classifications. In the United Kingdom, where a long tradition of craft-based unionism had led to trade union control over job content (although through established custom rather than legal status, as in the United States), job classifications were a repeated theme of collective bargaining, particularly during the 1970s (ILO, 1997, p. 113).

Faced with heightened global competition and the diffusion of lean production concepts, however, unions in these countries have begun to adopt more proactive policies on functional flexibility issues such as work reorganization and multi-skilling. A good example of this evolution of union policy can be found in the Canadian Autoworkers union (CAW). In 1989 the CAW adopted a formal "Statement on the Reorganization of Work" criticizing labour-management partnership approaches to workplace change. The statement referred to such initiatives as "management stratagems to replace worker solidarity with total identification with the goals of the company". But over the last five years or so, the CAW's hardline stance has begun to soften. In more recent agreements, the CAW has exhibited a more cooperative orientation, as it negotiated changes in areas such as training, technological change, work teams, flexible work scheduling, and product quality. In exchange for granting employers greater flexibility, it has been pushing for pay and employment gains.

In another shift in union policy, the restructuring of the American motor and steel industries in the 1980s led the major industrial unions to negotiate training programmes to assist the growing numbers of dislocated workers. These programmes, run by the United Steelworkers of America (USWA), the UAW, the International Association of Machinists (IAM) and others, were geared towards helping workers displaced by technological change to re-enter the workforce with more marketable skills. Training programmes such as these have helped facilitate the reorganization of work, while protecting workers' interests. In the process, new partnerships have been developed, departing from traditional "arm's-length" labour-management relations. For instance, the USWA developed a "New Direction" programme, leading to its first agreement with Inland Steel in 1993. It created a new labour-management partnership that provides for full workers' participation at all levels of the company, including the boardroom. The agreement also sought to restructure and modernize the company within a framework of employment security.

Trade unions in many European countries have traditionally been more favourable towards work reforms than their counterparts in the United Kingdom and North America. Dutch trade unions, for example, have usually taken a positive attitude towards such modern concepts of work organization. There is no tradition of "job control" in the Netherlands, so there was little resistance by skilled tradespeople against non-skilled workers taking over some of their tasks. Levels of payment are determined by widely supported schemes of job evaluation, which opens up the possibility that participating in teamwork may result in movement towards a higher pay scale. Bargaining on work organization issues mainly takes place between management and the works council at the enterprise level. German unions such as IG Metall, and to some extent the large public sector union (ÖTV), are engaged in further efforts to increase direct worker participation linked to a strategy of developing worker-friendly alternatives to "lean production" in the metal sector, and improving service quality and customer orientation in the public sector. These significant strategic and structural adjustments are taking place in the context of a movement to incorporate economic revitalization into broader areas of social concern, such as environmental issues. The chemical union (IG Chemie) has also intensified its efforts to build more workplace-level participation, albeit in a more reactive mode, and in the absence of alternative production strategies (Wever, 1997, p. 459).

In Latin American countries, as elsewhere, work organization has been regarded as management prerogative and is not usually a subject for collective bargaining. It should be noted, however, that innovative forms of work organization such as teamwork, as well as flexible working-time arrangements, became important points on the bargaining agendas of certain multinational companies in Latin America during the first half of the 1990s. For instance, unions and management at Volkswagen in Brazil have negotiated issues concerning teamwork (1997), out-sourcing (1991) and flexible working time (1996).

In Asia, while work organization has generally been outside the scope of collective bargaining in the Republic of Korea, trade unions in some large work-places have developed a sort of informal negotiation process on work organization issues such as the line speed, changes in production layout and job rotation. Yet as confrontational approaches were taken by both management and union representatives at the workplace, this informal negotiation failed to produce mutually beneficial solutions. This is why the revised law on labour-management councils (LMCs) in 1997 allows LMCs to discuss work organization issues. It also grants new co-determination rights concerning the in-house training of employees in order to channel informal negotiations on work organization into the cooperative forum of LMCs.

Although some observers argue that the existence of trade unions and collective bargaining can inhibit flexibility and change, evidence indicates that the presence of trade unions may in some cases facilitate work reforms. In Ireland, for example, a greater percentage of jobs in all categories, particularly manual and clerical, have become broader and more flexible in unionized firms over the last three years than in non-union firms. These findings are quite dramatic and probably indicate the extent to which trade unions have embraced the change agenda formulated by the ICTU and the Services, Industrial, Professional and Technical Union (SIPTU) over the last five years. A greater number of jobs have become more specific in organizations that do not recognize trade unions, which runs counter to the flexible firm predictions (Ireland country study). However, opposing evidence suggesting that unions discourage work reforms also exists. One study in the Republic of Korea suggests that job descriptions in unionized workplaces are less broad than those in non-unionized workplaces (K.S. Park, 1992, p. 184). This may be a result of defensive union strategies against management initiatives, brought on by the adversarial atmosphere of labour-management relations in the country. Indeed, as described in a recent ILO report, the most essential aspect is "that the diffusion of workplace level innovations is influenced less by the mere presence or absence of unions than by the actual role they play. When unions play a consultative role in decision-making the new practices expand more rapidly. This finding suggests that it is the quality of labour-management relationships and not the mere existence of a union that has a positive impact on the productivity of enterprises" (ILO, 1997, p. 100).

Factors affecting union policy

As noted earlier, trade unions in many countries have recently shifted their stance on labour market flexibility from a defensive policy towards a more proactive one. Most trade unions see the importance of making work more flexible as a means of creating jobs. Having been convinced of the economic inevitability of greater flexibilization, unions are cooperating actively with employers and their organizations in the creation of new work rules. To reiterate, a majority of trade unions are in favour of flexibility as long as decisions on flexibility and the methods of implementing it are not exclusively in the hands of the employer, but instead belong to a process of bipartite rule making. Unions in a number of countries have expressed this attitude, including those in Australia, Barbados, the Netherlands, Norway and the United Kingdom.

In some countries, however, rivalry among unions is preventing them from developing effective and proactive policies on labour market flexibility. In the Republic of Korea, bitter rivalries between the FKTU and the Korean Confederation of Trade Unions (KCTU) hindered these trade unions from pursuing pragmatic and proactive policies for negotiating new laws on labour market flexibility. In India, where a dozen trade unions sometimes coexist in the same workplace, collective agreements successfully concluded with some unions are often stalled before being implemented because of legal challenges brought by rival (often minority) unions. This is partly because contesting unions are afraid that any change in workplace arrangements might disturb the existing balance of power among unions. The strong ideological hold among the leftist unions in India added another difficulty to developing a more pragmatic approach to negotiations on flexibility issues. To a lesser extent, ideological divisions among French unions at the national level have been obstacles to formulating more effective union strategies.

In those countries where there has been a shift in trade union policies on labour market flexibility, union attitudes vary significantly depending on the concrete forms of flexibility in question. Unions are wary of changes that erode solidarity among their members. In particular, they are very much concerned about the spread of flexible employment contracts and the growing employment insecurity around the world, since these forms of flexibility pose a tremendous threat to their members' welfare. In general, unions (and workers) tend to support flexibility in work organization, especially if they see that it is designed to improve the organization's productivity and competitiveness, but they remain cautious about adopting other forms of flexibility in the workplace.

However, there are also differences in attitudes based on occupation, sector and the hierarchical order of union organizations. In general, trade unions representing high-skilled employees and professionals have been more active in promoting flexibility. The Federation of Norwegian Professional Associations (AF) has advocated increased wage flexibility (including the decentralization of wage negotiations) both in the public and private sectors, more so than the LO and the Confederation of Vocational Unions (YS). Likewise, the Swedish Confederation of Professional Employees (TCO) has recently modified its stance on flexible work, owing to the growing interest among its members in various forms of atypical work. TCO assumes that flexible work and spending more working time at home are practices that will spread. However, it is concerned with the fact that the normal rules governing the labour market do not completely cover these forms of work, most notably homeworking.

There also appear to be differences in policies pursued by trade unions at different levels. For example, the Canadian Autoworkers (CAW) at the national level initially took a very critical stance on work reorganization, distrusting employers' initiatives in this area. However, local CAW unions have increasingly adopted a cooperative approach to these managerial initiatives. Local unions tended to see a more direct link between cooperating with management and keeping the motor vehicle plant open and profitable, thus securing their members' jobs. This kind of vertical divergence of trade union attitudes has been noted in France, too. While the CGT and the FO have taken a determined stance on flexibility issues at the national level, their unions at the industry level have been more open to labour market flexibility. Indeed, more collective agreements on flexibility have been concluded by the CGT and FO local unions than those of the CFDT, although the latter is generally more favourable to flexibility at the national level.

More generally, the relationship between the level at which the locus of union power resides and the predominant attitude on labour market flexibility is a controversial issue. Employers and neo-liberal observers have often argued that a decentralized union structure is more likely to be instrumental in enhancing labour market flexibility than a centralized one. It is clear that, as the prevailing attitudes among Japanese enterprise unions indicate, a decentralized union structure is more likely to lead to the adoption of cooperative policies on enterprise flexibility because their members' welfare is directly linked to the firm's fortunes. This observation is in line with the earlier remark made on the relatively favourable attitudes of some CAW local unions to workplace flexibility, in comparison with those of their central body. A similar observation can be made about the attitudes of many works councils in Germany, compared to those of industrial unions.

Nevertheless, the most centralized trade unions in Ireland and Norway seem to have been highly successful in enhancing labour market flexibility. As noted earlier, the centralized union and bargaining structures in these countries have helped bring about economic recovery and good labour market performance. At the same time, it should be noted that strong central union power in Norway is combined with highly decentralized trade union functions: local bargaining at the firm level is an integral part of the negotiating system; a collective agreement usually has to be ratified by union members within the scope of the agreement; and local unions play an important role in co-determination, as well as safety and health at the firm level. Enterprise-level bargaining covers not only pay, but occupational safety and health, work organization, the development of company organizational structures and the introduction of new technology. Thus, Norway has a long tradition of negotiating productivity locally. Direct contracts between management and workers, and direct participation of workers in managerial decision-making mostly take place within the tradition of co-determination and are regarded as a supplement to, not a substitute for, representative participation. This tradition seems to have helped Norwegian trade unions adapt to the new environment.

The examples quoted above clearly indicate that the strength of a union at the decentralized level is a contributing factor to enhancing labour market flexibility at the micro level. However, it is also true that the advantages of a decentralized union structure do not rule out the importance of the contributions which centralized unions can make to labour market flexibility. Evidence indeed indicates that the complete delegation of union power to the enterprise level is not always conducive to unions' playing a greater role in enhancing enterprise flexibility. As discussed in Chapter 3, Australian unions at the local level appear to be having some trouble exercising the kind of leverage that was available to the central body (ACTU) through its national power base, and the diffusion of workplace reforms appears to have been hampered by the devolution of union power to the workplace level (Wever, 1997, p. 463). Thus, a balanced distribution of bargaining agendas and organizational power between the higher and lower levels of bargaining would be crucial for both the effective functioning of trade unions and better economic performance.

At the enterprise level, trade unions' approach to enterprise flexibility largely depends on the quality of labour-management relations and the managerial philosophy prevailing in the firm. When management recognizes the union as an equal partner and maintains open communication and consultation at all levels of the organization, unions tend to cooperate fully with management in introducing flexible work arrangements. Proof of this can be found not only in industrialized countries, but in newly industrializing and developing countries as well, including at LG Electronics in the Republic of Korea and at a top steel maker in the Philippines. On the contrary, when management tries to avoid or repress the unions' collective voice, unions are likely to become suspicious of management campaign for a flexible workplace, in case it is designed to weaken the union – as shown in Hyundai Motor Company in the Republic of Korea and in many workplaces in India.

The growing role of works councils, and how unions view it

The growing focus of industrial relations on enterprise flexibility has created an increasing role for works councils in many countries. With few exceptions, employers in most countries have expressed a clear preference for home-made deals with the works councils to solutions negotiated with unions at higher levels. Many governments are also encouraging the institution of works councils with a view to creating more cooperative approaches to newly emerging qualitative issues. Recent legislation in the Republic of Korea, for example, broadened the agenda for consultation through labour-management councils to cover work organization, and added new subjects for co-determination including job training and employees' welfare.

Although trade unions do not usually oppose the intrusion of works councils into flexibility matters, they tend to take a cautious approach to the issue. Some unions, including those in the Netherlands, have been suspicious about the growing importance of works councils in regulating employment conditions because they might undermine unions' essential functions. In countries such as the United States, where labour-management relations have traditionally been adversarial and union avoidance strategies are common, trade unions tend to oppose any attempts to institutionalize alternative employees' representation. From the unions' point of view, works councils have a weakness in that they find it difficult to counter proposals offering short-term advantages to incumbent employees (insiders) instead of employment opportunities to unemployed workers (outsiders). Moreover, it is often difficult for works councils to resist employers' insistence on introducing certain changes (e.g. flexible working-time arrangements) that are undesirable from the workers' viewpoint, if the employers hint at possible consequences for job security in the event that the works council rejects the overall plan. On the other hand, in countries such as Japan and the Republic of Korea where labour-management committees tend to be represented by union leaders, there has been little contest between unions and other channels of employees' representation. And since works councils in Italy are highly unionized, it is difficult to identify any difference between their conception of flexibility and that advanced by the unions. Nevertheless, works councillors in Italy, being more in touch with the rank-and-file, appear more willing to experiment with new work formulas (Italy country study). In general, trade unions in many countries argue that the role of works councils can only be supplementary to collective bargaining. Dutch unions have succeeded in setting a new demarcation line between trade unions and works councils through the new Works Council Act of 1997. The Act gives works councils the right to negotiate with employers on employment conditions and to conclude "company agreements". However, these agreements can only include matters that are not settled by collective contracts or need to be specified for the individual enterprise. This ensures the primacy of collective bargaining, while in sectors or enterprises where collective agreements are absent, the works council has the right to negotiate with the employer.

Works councils themselves are also encountering difficulties. In Germany, for example, they are confronted with a growing number of negotiation duties, which they had not assumed before. Moreover, the spread of new forms of work organization such as teamwork and direct participation schemes such as quality control circles can pose a threat to the indirect participation mechanism of works councils, although reports show that indirect and direct channels of participation complement one another in both Sweden and Germany (Berggren, 1992, and Murakami, 1995).

In some countries, the system of employees' representation through works councils has met with opposition from both unions and employers. In India, for example, the participative forums were seen by unions as a possible infringement of their collective bargaining rights and managers did not want to give up their right to manage. Indian trade unions are also insisting that participation should begin at the top (board level), while management prefers a bottom-up (shop-floor participation) approach (India country study). Workers tend to see this participative channel as another bargaining forum or grievance channel. In the sphere of workers' involvement and participation, the major shift is in terms of a pronounced preference for the "new human resource policies" for employee participation, rather than union participation, and encouragement of small-group activities that emphasize problem solving over preoccupation with individual or collective grievances in the participative forums. Sodhi's study confirms this: 68 per cent of the 84 sample firms had employees' participation in problem solving in 1993, as against 46 per cent in 1983 (Sodhi, 1995, cited in the India country study).

Concluding remarks

The response of the social partners to labour market flexibility has varied greatly across countries, sectors and hierarchical orders of an organization. Not surprisingly, trade unions and employers have widely differing views on the issue of flexibility, although there are some signs of convergence. For their part, trade unions are gradually conceding the need to enhance labour market flexibility as a means of coping with high unemployment, although they caution that the flexibilization process normally exacts a heavy toll on workers, particularly in terms of employment security. Employers, who have been a driving force behind labour market flexibility, have had to temper their zeal for change somewhat because they often find it difficult to enhance competitiveness without enlisting the support of employees. None the less, how best to harmonize the need for better, more stable employment conditions with the pursuit of flexible employment relations remains a key point of conflict and compromise between trade unions and employers.

OUTCOMES OF NEGOTIATIONS OVER FLEXIBILITY 5

Introduction

The flexibilization of the labour market which has occurred over the last ten to 15 years has required sacrifices on the part of workers. Depending on the types of flexibility sought, these sacrifices have mainly consisted of the need, for many workers, to accept a significant decrease in their employment security, a notable weakening of their income security and a constant adjustment to changing – and often increasingly uncomfortable – working and living conditions. The most difficult sacrifices for workers are undoubtedly those which concern their employment security. This is indeed a highly sensitive issue for any worker, even in instances where there is no complete job loss involved or when the difficulties – whatever they may be – prove eventually to be of a temporary nature.

It is only natural that workers would expect quid pro quos (or trade-offs) in exchange for the concessions requested of them. The purpose of this chapter is to provide a brief overview of the main types of these quid pro quos. The overview will be limited to instances where the trade-offs have been the result of a bargaining process. The reason is that bargaining is essentially an instrument for striking compromises and trade-offs are therefore most likely to occur if the flexibilization of the labour market has been achieved through bargaining. The concept of "bargaining" will, however, be taken in its widest sense – namely to include all forms of bipartite and tripartite negotiations or consultations, irrespective of the level at which they take place. The instances thus covered range from the most formal to the most informal types of negotiations and consultations. An example of informal types of consultations and negotiations are the unofficial contacts which take place in many countries among the government and the central employers' and workers' organizations in the course of drafting new legislation.

This chapter is composed of three sections. The first will propose a number of general considerations concerning trade-offs in flexibility bargaining, and will argue that an important criterion for categorizing these trade-offs is the level at which they have been negotiated. Consequently, the second and third sections will deal successively with the trade-offs that have been negotiated above the enterprise level (mainly the central, but also the sectoral and regional levels) and at the enterprise level.

Some basic issues concerning trade-offs in flexibility bargaining

The purpose of this section is to provide a background to the two following sections. Its aim is, more precisely, to enable readers to place the examples of trade-offs given in these two sections into a broader perspective, so as to make it easier to assess their nature, scope and potential impact. While the information provided in these sections should therefore be read in the light of the considerations proposed in this section, the reverse is equally necessary. The present section is bound to include a number of generalizations and simplifications which will have to be complemented by the examples included in the following sections in order to allow an accurate assessment of the prevailing situations.

This section includes two sets of considerations. These will be successively concerned with the basic difficulties that have affected all give-and-take processes in flexibility bargaining and the basic differences that exist between the trade-offs that have been negotiated respectively at the levels above the enterprise and at the enterprise level.

The give-and-take processes that have taken place in the course of flexibility bargaining have proved very difficult, particularly for workers. This is principally due to the fact that the flexibilization of the labour market has occurred in – and has probably been prompted to a large extent by – a context which is mainly characterized by sharply increased national and international competition and by slow economic growth, if not economic recession. Other factors, such as mounting pressures on management to deliver higher short-term returns to shareholders and the deregulation of national and international financial markets, have also made it difficult for management and workers to achieve workable trade-offs while bargaining over flexibility issues.

As a consequence of this environment, the flexibilization of the labour market has led to a significant erosion of workers' rights in fundamentally important areas which concern their employment and income security and the (relative) stability of their working and living conditions. Regarding the trade-offs arising from flexibility bargaining, there has not been an attempt to negotiate completely "new" types of trade-offs, as such an approach would imply an attempt to drastically change the present paradigms of economic and social policy. As an example of such change, one could think of the introduction of a basic income guarantee for all citizens, based on the belief that it will never again be possible to achieve full employment. In fact, the trade-offs actually negotiated in flexibility bargaining do not reflect such boldly innovative approaches. Instead, they appear to be fundamentally in line with the traditional paradigms, in so far as their basic objective is still to perpetuate a situation where everybody can, in principle, earn a living through work (and where minimum compensation is offered to those who cannot find work).

It must, however, be added that while the trade-offs are basically compatible with the traditional paradigms, some are nevertheless more innovative than others. At one end of the spectrum are arrangements aimed at averting the erosion of workers' rights. An extreme example would be that where planned redundancies have been totally or partly avoided – possibly after a strike – for a certain period of time, or where moderate wage increases have been granted – possibly also after a strike – in spite of the employers' initial intention to impose a wage freeze. In such cases, there is actually not much of a trade-off, at least in so far as the quid pro quo obtained by the workers is in the same area as the initial employers' claim and has simply consisted of the rejection or curtailment of this claim. Higher up in the spectrum are increasingly complex arrangements which still pursue the objective mentioned earlier (i.e. to perpetuate a situation where everybody can, in principle, earn his livelihood through work), but as a longer-term objective and through a – preferably broad and varied – set of predominantly indirect measures. Examples of such arrangements would be the combined recourse to reduced hours, increased working-time flexibility, increased part-time work and greater skill flexibility in exchange for the protection or creation of employment. Another example would be the establishment of an overall framework intended to facilitate medium-term employment creation through macroeconomic policy measures, changes in education and training systems, flexibilization of the labour law and improvements in the system of social protection. As will be seen in the next section, central – or at least sectoral – agreements are often needed to establish such frameworks. However, at the end of this chapter we also mention a few cases where such policies have been implemented at the enterprise level (see pp. 162-164).

Regarding the main differences between the trade-offs negotiated at the levels above the enterprise and at the enterprise level, one must recall that the flexibilization of the labour market was bound to go hand in hand – and has actually done so – with a significant decentralization of industrial relations in all the countries where these systems were traditionally rather centralized. Because enterprises have increasingly needed tailor-made solutions to their problems in order to remain competitive in national and international markets, they have gradually become the only place where both the flexibilization measures themselves and the corresponding trade-offs could be translated into precise commitments for either party. In many cases, the provisions of sectoral and central agreements were simply too vague and general to be of any real interest to enterprises. Trade unions have also become increasingly reluctant over the years to accept labour market flexibilization through sectoral and central agreements because the employers' organizations which were parties to these agreements were not in a position to make genuine commitments on behalf of their members regarding employment protection or creation and, therefore, were unable to offer any real trade-offs in exchange for flexibility measures.

There is undoubtedly much truth in these criticisms of higher-level agreements. However, it must be emphasized that if enterprise agreements offer certain potentialities which higher-level agreements do not, the reverse is equally true. First, higher-level agreements – particularly central agreements – can deal with dimensions of labour market flexibilization which are clearly beyond the reach of any single enterprise. As mentioned earlier, such agreements can establish an overall framework conducive to employment creation through macroeconomic policy measures, changes in the education and training systems, and changes in social and labour legislation. Second, higher-level agreements make it possible to conduct both coordinated and solidaristic policies (i.e. policies behind which there is a global concept and which ensure a certain degree of solidarity in the solutions to the problems dealt with, thereby minimizing inequalities and social exclusion). This is illustrated by the fact that many higher-level agreements aim at promoting the employ-ability of as many workers as possible in a medium-term perspective, whereas some enterprise agreements aim at maintaining existing jobs in a short-term perspective.

This is not to imply that certain bargaining levels are better than others for flexibility bargaining. It is rather that each level has its specific potentialities, and that these are complementary. While enterprise-level bargaining is indispensable to work out the concrete solutions needed at that level, higher-level bargaining can add a number of valuable dimensions to flexibility bargaining. Even if higher-level bargaining has only rarely had a direct impact on employment creation – which is a key trade-off in flexibility bargaining – it has often changed perceptions and altered principles, thereby making way for alternative solutions at lower levels (ILO, 1997, pp. 131-132). To the extent that higher-level bargaining is tripartite, it also allows both market forces and the public authorities to exert their influences, thus avoiding both excessive state control and excessive liberalism, while bridging the areas of competence of the State and of the other two social partners (ILO, 1996, p. 30).

Trade-offs at levels above the enterprise

This section gives some examples of trade-offs negotiated at the higher levels in order to allow a better understanding of the general considerations involved. A distinction will be made between trade-offs negotiated at the central level and at the sectoral level.

Trade-offs at the central level

In countries where central negotiations and consultations – whether bipartite or tripartite – play an important role, they generally cover five broad subject areas, which are closely interlinked (ILO, 1997, p. 130). The first involves measures intended to promote macroeconomic stability, consisting primarily of provisions seeking to moderate wage costs, together with provisions regarding budgetary, fiscal and monetary policies. The second includes measures aimed at enhancing the flexibility of the labour market, with working-time flexibility being the most frequently cited topic, although there are also numerous provisions to increase flexibility in the individual employment relationship, as well as wages and work organization. The third revolves around combating unemployment and creating jobs, primarily involving measures connected with training, redistributing work, integrating unemployed workers into employment (for example, by means of training courses or subsidized contracts) and tapping sources of employment (for example, through local and community development, and neighbourhood services). The fourth and fifth involve respectively the reform of social security and social welfare systems – mainly with a view to decreasing their costs – and measures aimed at supporting economic activity.

The main differences between countries in the ways they deal with these issues do not lie in the substantive solutions to the issues concerned. This means, in other words, that no country sets itself apart with solutions that are fundamentally different from – and, possibly, much more efficient than – those adopted by others (in which case, it might be noted in passing, the latter countries would immediately have attempted to copy the former). Instead, the main differences lie in the more or less comprehensive way in which the various issues are dealt with. Since this is obviously a question of degree, it is impossible to establish a clear-cut distinction between countries that follow a broad approach and those that do not. It is nevertheless clear that while some countries tend to deal with a great number of issues and consider all of them at the same time in overall package-deal consultations or negotiations, others tend to cover a more limited number of issues and to consider them separately. The trade-off is obviously more apparent in the former countries, but this does not mean that there is no trade-off between formally separate consultations or negotiations in the latter countries. The following paragraphs provide a few examples of each approach.

A good example of a broad package-deal arrangement is the Italian tripartite accord of July 1993 (Italy country study). As mentioned in Chapter 3, the "Social Pact" is principally aimed at introducing – as part of a (limited) incomes policy – a non-inflationary wages policy incorporated in a process of central tripartite consultations and at flexibilizing the labour market in a way acceptable to all parties. The agreement provides that two tripartite meetings will take place every year in May and June, and again in September. At the May and June meetings, the Government will disclose its budgetary objectives for the period before presenting its three-year Economic and Financial Planning Document. The purpose of the meeting is to develop jointly agreed targets for inflation, GDP growth and employment. The September meeting is part of the budget process, and its conclusions are to be transposed in the annual Finance Bill.

The wage policy, which is an outcome of these tripartite consultations, is based on the projected inflation rate. In order to ensure the success of this policy – and, more generally, to guarantee an orderly development of the whole bargaining process – the July 1993 agreement introduces a sophisticated system of articulated bargaining which provides for a distribution of issues among the various bargaining levels (central, sectoral and enterprise), as well as the timing of the negotiations to take place at each level. According to these provisions, wage increases are basically agreed upon at the sectoral level, with the amounts depending on the inflation forecasts established through central tripartite discussions. Additional increases may be agreed upon at the enterprise level, but only if they can be financed through productivity improvements achieved at that level. The central agreement also provides for a system of provisional wage adjustments at the sectoral level, in case sectoral bargaining cannot be completed within the allotted time span. Furthermore, it includes precise clauses on how sectoral wages should be adjusted if the inflation forecasts on which they are based prove to be wrong. The provisions of the 1993 central agreement related to wage policy and to the structure and operation of the national bargaining system are generally considered as having lived up to their objectives. These objectives were quite ambitious in the Italian context, particularly because they entailed suppressing the system of automatic wage indexation on past inflation, which had been a "taboo" in Italy for many decades.

The central Italian agreement of 1993 also included a number of measures aimed at overcoming what was widely regarded as excessive regulation of the formal Italian labour market. Trade unions and employers were encouraged to agree, with the help of the regions and the employment agencies, on broad packages of measures capable of remedying the situation. Since this part of the

1993 agreement was not considered particularly successful, it was complemented by another central tripartite agreement in 1996. The latter agreement is not limited to issues of flexibility, but takes a comprehensive approach to reform. Since it includes a great number of provisions of a highly technical nature, it is not possible to give a detailed overview of its contents here. Suffice it to say that it deals with such varied issues as reforming education and training systems, and the social welfare system, reducing working time, labour market reforms in such areas as employment agencies, apprenticeship contracts and temporary work, and regional growth and employment creation through local and community development.

The most basic characteristics of the Italian agreements are, first, that the agreements do not merely aim at specific labour market reforms, but also at creating an overall environment conducive to such reforms and, second, that both objectives are being pursued through many measures carefully balanced against one another so as to achieve an overall compromise between the interests of all parties involved.

These basic characteristics of the Italian agreements can also be found in several agreements concluded in other countries. Among the many examples – most of which were, not surprisingly, concluded in Western Europe, because of the deeply rooted tradition of central bargaining in many countries of this region – mention can be made of those concluded in Ireland, Belgium and the Netherlands. As already described in Chapter 3, the predominant feature of Irish industrial relations since 1987 has been a series of centrally negotiated tripartite, three-year pacts which have covered broad economic and social issues (Ireland country study). While the first agreement focused on moderate pay increases in an attempt to improve economic performance and reduce unemployment, the three following ones addressed significantly wider concerns. Except for specific wage increases, these three agreements do not enumerate the trade-offs in very precise terms, but place the main emphasis on broad policy statements to indicate the unity among the social partners in addressing economic and social challenges. The most recent agreement, concluded in 1997 and called "Partnership 2000", makes the following statement with regard to the relationship between social cohesion and competitiveness:

Competitiveness is determined by relative performance on pay, taxes and public expenditure but also, and equally, by other factors such as productivity, innovation, education and training and the cost and quality provided by the State and state-sponsored bodies. Improvements in social solidarity and increased social inclusion make an important contribution to sustaining competitiveness and society's overall efficiency and cohesion. The challenge that this Partnership faces is to make competitiveness and social solidarity self-sustaining. The challenge of global competition and the information society requires continuous innovation, flexible working methods, highly skilled workers and lifelong learning.

In accordance with this statement, the agreement includes a series of provisions intended both to maintain the country's financial equilibrium and to ensure a fair distribution of the fruits of growth in such a way as to benefit the most disadvantaged groups, particularly the unemployed. To this end, it recommends a policy of modest pay increases and a number of more concrete measures aimed at increasing competitiveness through increased labour market flexibility.

In Belgium, an important tripartite draft agreement was negotiated in 1996 (Belgium country study). Although it was not ratified by one of the two most important trade unions, and thus had to be implemented through legislation, it is worth noting that, like the Italian agreement, the Belgian draft agreement included ambitious sections on wages and incomes policy, and on labour market flexibility. As regards wages, the draft agreement made provision for increases in remuneration to be maintained, through a complex system of articulated bargaining, within a bracket extending from the increase in the cost of living in Belgium as a minimum to the average wage increases in France, Germany and the Netherlands (Belgium's three most direct competitors) as a maximum. The part of the draft agreement devoted to labour market flexibility includes many highly technical measures. All provisions, whether they concern wages or labour market flexibility, are closely interconnected in so far as each of them constitutes an integral part of a broad compromise resulting from long and difficult negotiations.

In the Netherlands, the global trade-off that has decisively inspired national economic and social policies up to the present day was initiated in the 1982 Wassenaar agreement, referred to in Chapter 3, in which the workers accepted far-reaching sacrifices in wages and benefits in exchange for job creation measures (the Netherlands country study). A number of important joint documents on various aspects of labour market flexibility, which are clearly in the wake of the Wassenaar agreement, were adopted more recently. The most significant examples are a policy document entitled "The New Way", adopted in 1993, as well as an advice on flexibility and security, adopted in 1996. These very complex documents clearly reflect attempts towards a new approach, in which flexibility and security are considered as complementary rather than opposing concepts. Thus, the basic aim of the 1996 advice was both to make individual employment relationships more flexible and to offer a reasonable degree of protection and stability to the workers who are parties to such relationships.

France, on the other hand, follows a less global approach (France country study). The French social partners are not used to the types of "social pacts" that are frequently negotiated in other Western European countries with a view to providing package-deal solutions to the major economic and social problems of the day. The only exceptions are a few select agreements, such as the "Grenelle agreements" of 1968, which were negotiated on an ad hoc basis to put an end to lengthy general strikes. This does not mean, however, that there is no central bargaining in France. In fact, such bargaining takes place quite frequently, but each central agreement tends to be limited to one clearly identified subject.

Examples of such agreements include those on vocational training in 1994, working time in 1995, and entry of young people into working life in 1995, and the three agreements in 1996 on financing complementary pensions. Although there are no formal quid pro quos between these agreements, there are nevertheless certain implicit trade-offs. This is due to the fact that in countries where the social partners are used to consulting one another on major issues of national economic and social policy, all these issues will unavoidably be seen in their global context. Under those circumstances, it is most unlikely that the overall outcome of these central dealings will be heavily weighted in favour of – or against – one party. Instead, it is much more likely that a sort of global trade-off will continuously be achieved in the course of these dealings, even if this generally happens in an informal and non-explicit manner.

In addition, a number of the French central agreements have been built around their own specific trade-offs. One of the best examples is the 1995 agreement on working time. Although this agreement did not break new ground in terms of concrete measures, it was nevertheless a breakthrough in that, after long and sterile discussions on the issue of working time, it addressed a new message to the negotiators' constituents with a view to subsequent negotiations at the sectoral or enterprise level: contrary to previously held positions, the central trade unions signalled that they were no longer opposed to more flexible working-time arrangements, whereas the central employers' organization (the NPF) recognized that the reduction of working hours might be a means of creating jobs and reminded enterprises that they should take an active part in combating unemployment (ILO, 1997, pp. 122–123).

The situation currently prevailing in Spain resembles the French situation in certain respects (Spain country study). In the early eighties, the Spanish social partners had attempted to follow a somewhat global approach and had succeeded in signing several broad central agreements, the most important of which was the 1984 Economic and Social Pact. In the late eighties and early nineties, encompassing central negotiations became increasingly difficult, and frequently resulted in failures. Thus a government-promoted attempt at negotiating a new social pact failed in 1994, which led to largely unilateral action by the Government. In order to avoid a repetition of this scenario, renewed efforts were undertaken by the parties to revive central negotiations. These efforts were successful in so far as they recently led to the signing of a number of central agreements dealing with more limited subjects, such as safety and health, the settlement of labour disputes and job stability. As in France, there is an implicit attempt to achieve a global trade-off through the central bargaining process as a whole. In addition, some of the central agreements represent in themselves a well-balanced compromise between the signatory parties on the specific issue dealt with in the agreement. This is true, for example, of the agreement on job stability, where the main trade-off was that the traditionally heavy restrictions on redundancy in permanent contracts – which had led employers to recruit, wherever possible, under fixed-term contracts – would be lightened and that the employers would, as a quid pro quo, increasingly recruit under permanent contracts (ILO, 1997, p. 132).

Trade-offs at the sectoral level

As mentioned earlier, sectoral bargaining remains an important component of most national industrial relations systems in which it has played a substantial role in the past (particularly with respect to Western Europe). With the exception of a few countries, such as the United Kingdom, sectoral agreements continue to be concluded on a regular basis. None the less, the nature of sectoral bargaining has changed considerably over the last 20 to 30 years, mainly in that sectoral agreements now grant more leeway to enterprise bargaining than was the case in the past. Again, the driving force behind this change is mounting competitive pressures, which are causing enterprises to find tailor-made solutions to their problems. Such solutions often require more precise commitments from the parties than those that can be defined at the sectoral level. All this has led to more flexible formulations of the clauses in sectoral agreements and, at times, to the inclusion of opening clauses in these agreements, as discussed in Chapter 3.

Furthermore, current sectoral bargaining resembles central bargaining in certain respects and differs from it in others. Like central bargaining, it can – at least in the sector concerned – promote coordinated and solidaristic policies, and open the way for new solutions to be adopted at the enterprise level. In many instances, sectoral bargaining will play this twofold role within a framework previously established by a central agreement. Regarding the differences between central and sectoral bargaining, it must first be mentioned that the latter is unable – or, at least, is less able than the former – to deal with such key issues as national macroeconomic policies. Another difference between the two levels of bargaining concerns the extent to which they are able to provide precise solutions to the problems dealt with and to define precise commitments for the parties: in these areas, the potential of sectoral bargaining is clearly greater than that of central bargaining, although it still remains considerably more limited than that of enterprise bargaining.

Sectoral bargaining in Western Europe focuses primarily on job saving – particularly through wage moderation and changes in working time – this term being taken in its broadest possible sense. Concerning working time, it should be pointed out that, some years ago, attempts were made in a number of countries to achieve substantial reductions in working hours so as to optimize the potential of the reforms to create jobs. Examples include some of the sectoral agreements concluded in France in the wake of the central agreement of 1993, mentioned earlier. Another example is the 1994 agreement in the German metal sector, which encouraged enterprises to reduce weekly working time from 36 to 30 hours, with a proportional cut in wages, in exchange for a commitment to freeze layoffs during the term of the agreement. The eventual impact of these agreements has, however, been rather limited. This relative lack of success is due to specific difficulties, namely the inability of employers' organizations to make precise commitments on behalf of their members in terms of protecting or creating employment, and the subsequent reluctance of the trade unions to make substantial concessions. This is probably the main reason why the parties have tended to revert to the more traditional practice of relatively small reductions in working time and relatively small concessions in terms of wages and flexibility (ILO, 1997, pp. 123–124). One exception, however, is France's Aubray Law, adopted in 1998, which paves the way for a 35-hour work week (down from 39) by the year 2000, with the primary objective of creating or preserving jobs through a reduction in working time.

Among the many examples of sectoral trade-offs, those achieved in Germany no doubt spark the greatest interest (Germany country study). The reasons are, first, that sectoral bargaining plays a more important role in Germany than in many other countries and, second, that this role has recently been challenged to a greater extent in that country than elsewhere. At present, the most common trade-offs in Germany are those built around relatively limited wage moderation (concerning both regular wages and bonuses), relatively limited reductions in working time and increased working-time flexibility. Several clauses concerning working time, for example, allow deviations from the standard weekly hours at the enterprise level under certain conditions and within certain limits. Thus, an agreement signed in 1993 in the chemical industry allows for fluctuations in the weekly working time of plus or minus two hours from the standard 37.5 hour working week, provided that there is an agreement with the works council or the trade union at the enterprise level. In 1994, these parameters were extended by an additional half-hour, so as to create a "corridor" extending from 35 to 40 hours. Other clauses provide that work on Saturday and Sunday will no longer be paid as overtime. This is the case, for example, in an agreement concluded in the textile industry in 1996. Still other clauses, which can be found in various sectors, provide that overtime will, to the extent possible, be compensated with time off.

These trade-offs achieved in Germany are not very different from those achieved in other countries. Examples of less common quid pro quos can, however, be found in the chemical industry. In this sector, the parties agreed in 1997 to allow a reduction in basic remuneration of up to 10 per cent through enterprise agreements in order to secure employment or to increase efficiency. The agreements in the chemical industry include clauses regarding employment protection or creation by employers which are remarkably precise for a sectoral agreement. One of these agreements provides, for example, that employers "reckon on" a 5 per cent increase in apprenticeship contracts during the term of the agreement and that they "expect" to be in a position to turn 15 per cent of the fixed-term contracts due to expire during the term of the agreement into open-ended contracts. Another agreement is accompanied by an "Employers' Declaration on Employment" which states that the employers "expect" that the total volume of employment in the sector will not diminish from such date onwards and will, on average, be kept at the level so reached until such other date. These clauses go about as far as any at the sectoral level in terms of employment trade-offs.

Trade-offs at the enterprise level

As already discussed, flexibilization of the labour market has gone hand in hand with the move towards decentralizing collective bargaining. For this reason, most bargaining over flexibility has occurred at the enterprise level. Enterprise-level bargaining is more amenable to introducing flexibility because it enables the parties to adopt changes that respond to the specific needs of the enterprise and the workers.

The diversity of outcomes in enterprise-level bargaining, however, offers the challenge of how to present this information is a meaningful way. Therefore, this section attempts to group the myriad of trade-offs that have occurred at the enterprise level into one of four primary categories. The categories are as follows:

- trade-offs over job security;
- trade-offs over redundancy alternatives;
- trade-offs over working time;
- trade-offs over workers' lifestyles.

These groupings are somewhat artificial in that there is considerable overlap among the different categories. Nearly all trade-offs, for example, involve some element of job security and retention in exchange for greater flexibilization. However, the aim is to highlight the main areas in which trade-offs have occurred. An additional section on trade-offs in other areas covers employment contracts, wages and work organization, where trade-offs have been less common.

Trade-offs over job security

Technological progress and liberalization of trade in goods and services have brought ever more businesses into competition with one another. As a result, employers have begun experimenting with all kinds of flexible working arrangements with the aim of increasing their firms' competitive position, either through cutting costs or through improving productivity.

When attempting to cut costs, an employer often looks to ways to trim personnel expenditure. This can take the form of employee layoffs, wage cuts, wage freezes, lower overtime payments, or reduced non-wage labour costs such as health insurance and other social security benefits. But employers cannot simply impose these kinds of cost-cutting initiatives on a unionized workforce – they must be negotiated. The collective bargaining process forces each side to come up with trade-offs, which often result in granting employers more flexibility in holding down labour costs in exchange for granting workers more job security.

Job security is a paramount concern of workers the world over, one that naturally mounts when the prospect of change is introduced into the workplace. Change engenders a great deal of uncertainty and insecurity. In order to cope with these uncertainties, workers often seek guarantees that their jobs will be protected. Frequently, the only way that they will go along with changes in hours of work, compensation, the way their work is organized, or employment contracts is if their employer is willing to offer them assurances of job security in exchange. For these reasons, job security emerges as the primary trade-off under flexibility bargaining. The following are some specific examples of trade-offs over job security gleaned from the country studies.

Wage restraint for job security

Trade unions in the Republic of Korea, for example, have been willing to accept wage freezes and limited wage demands in exchange for greater job security and stability. As of May 1997, wage freezes had been adopted at 323 companies, and 173 unions had accepted wage determination without wage negotiations – increases of 200 and 600 per cent over the same period the previous year. This change in focus has been brought about, in part, by the fact that some large companies have begun announcing major lay-offs. As a result, job security emerged as the dominant theme in the Republic of Korea's collective bargaining for 1997.

A number of recent agreements in Germany have also traded wage restraint for greater job security. Certain industries suffering from competitive pressures have agreed to allow individual enterprises to deviate from the wage settlements concluded at the branch level. In the construction industry, for example, the parties agreed to let enterprises in hard-pressed eastern Germany reduce the remuneration package by up to 10 per cent in order to secure employment, improve competitiveness and strengthen the regional construction business. The same approach was followed in the chemical industry in western Germany, where up to a 10 per cent reduction in the collectively agreed wage provisions was granted in order to secure employment and improve competitiveness.

A similar situation has emerged in Argentina, where enterprise-level agreements have conceded reductions in wage increases negotiated at the branch level in exchange for maintaining employment. For example, at Massalin Particulares, S.A., a major tobacco company, the union agreed to a reduction of 10 to 20 per cent of the salary increase negotiated at the branch level as a means of ensuring job security. Each worker was willing to accept the sacrifice in order to forestall the need for lay-offs or other reductions in force in the near future.

Skill flexibility for job security

Unions in Japan have fought hard to establish the general understanding of employment security for core workers, and have had to agree to numerous trade-offs to achieve this objective. Most notably, the emphasis on employment security has created the need for skill flexibility among the regular workforce. This has been accomplished most effectively by capability-based compensation and employers' assessment of employees' development, to which Japanese unions gave tacit approval in exchange for promises of employment security (Japan country study).

This growing practice of employers' assessment of employees' development involves sorting workers according to their performance and potential into segments with different levels of employment security. At Sumitomo Rubber, for example, new recruits are designated, at the time of hire, to one of two career tracks – specialist or general management – on the basis of management's judgement and employees' preference. Specialist positions typically carry weaker employment protection than general management, so it was the firm's intention to identify those with less employment security very early in their tenure. As a result, the employer was limiting job security to a pre-selected segment of the workforce (ibid.).

Contingent work for job security

Managers have also sought to reduce labour costs by hiring temporary or contract workers – who often earn lower wages and benefits than regular workers. As discussed in Chapter 4, unions are generally opposed to the proliferation of non-standard workers as they often prove difficult to organize and can generate a downward pressure on the wages and benefits of the core workforce. As a trade-off for accepting more temporary and contract workers, unions have demanded limits on their numbers, or requirements that they automatically become part of the bargaining unit within a certain period of time. Contingent workers have also been accepted as a trade-off for greater job security for core workers.

Contingent workers offer a great deal of flexibility to employers, particularly when it comes to downsizing the workforce. Due to the temporary nature of their jobs, they can readily be hired or fired depending on the workload. The ease with which these contingent workers can be shed, ironically, can provide greater stability and protection for the core workforce.

In the United Kingdom, for example, an agreement reached at Agco in 1990 traded contingent work for job security. Under the terms of the agreement, new recruits to the manual workforce were taken on a fixed-term contract (FTC) basis, usually lasting 13 weeks in order to protect the core workers from being laid off. To allay the union's concerns that the temporary workers might be used to replace the core staff, the agreement provided an assurance that FTCs could not exceed 15 per cent of the total workforce. Furthermore, the FTCs could only be renewed for up to two years, at which point these workers either had to be made permanent or released.

So far, the agreement has proved beneficial to both employer and workers. Not only have the core workers been protected from lay-offs, but a number of workers on FTCs have become part of the permanent staff. The company enjoyed steady growth from 1990 to 1997, with the workforce expanding from 1,040 workers to 1,400 over this period. As a result, 230 FTC staff have been made permanent.

Cuts in working time for job security

For companies running into financial difficulties, flexibility bargaining often seeks alternatives to lay-offs. One solution reached in France was to reduce working hours and pay, in exchange for a promise of no forced redundancies throughout the term of the contract.

Sextant Avionique, a French aeronautics company, reached an agreement with its unions in 1993 calling for a reduction in weekly working time of 1 hour 30 minutes, with additional reductions of up to 2 hours 30 minutes possible at individual sites. The working-time reduction would be accumulated into nine working days per year, during which the establishment would close. Employees would be compensated for the time not worked at the rate of 60 per cent of net pay, made possible by a "compensated long-term, short-time working" scheme. According to the scheme, employers would pay 23 percentage points out of the 60 per cent net pay, with the remaining 37 percentage points paid by the Government. The overall effect of the plan is that workers would receive a 2 per cent reduction in monthly pay in exchange for working nine fewer days per year.

Another element of the plan was to encourage workers to voluntarily switch to half-time employment for two years, with a guaranteed income of 70 per cent of previous pay. Those choosing this option were also given an incentive bonus, equivalent to about US$5,000. Other alternatives included incentives for workers to take early retirement or unpaid long-term leave. The combined effects of these measures enabled the company to cut costs without having to resort to lay-offs.

Trade-offs over redundancy alternatives

This category – trade-offs over redundancy alternatives – is closely related to the preceding one – trade-offs over job security. However, there is an important distinction between the two. The first involved trade-offs intended to secure jobs for the future, in cases where an immediate threat of job losses was less likely. The second, however, concerns trade-offs that arise in the course of rescuing a firm from financial collapse and preventing the dissolution of its workforce. Under these situations, mass lay-offs or the closure of the enterprise are often imminent. The trade-offs typically involve finding creative means of keeping an enterprise in operation and its workforce employed.

As will be demonstrated, the types of trade-offs involved differ considerably when the life of an enterprise is at stake, as workers typically have to make greater concessions in order to keep their jobs. Understandably, the higher the stakes, the greater the trade-offs. When the continued existence of a company is involved – and workers' jobs hang in the balance – workers are often willing to agree to terms and conditions that would be unacceptable under less dire circumstances. While lay-offs or wage cuts are often unavoidable, the goal is to keep such draconian measures to a minimum. Hence, trade-offs over redundancy alternatives often focus on innovative solutions to restoring a firm's profitability and securing employment levels. The success of these endeavours, however, depends largely on the willingness of the parties involved to take short-term risks in order to achieve long-term gains.

Employee ownership for securing jobs

One innovative alternative to the closure of an enterprise or mass lay-offs is an employee-ownership scheme. In these situations, employees band together to purchase an interest in a failing enterprise in order to prevent it from going out of business.

This was the case in Germany, for example, where employees recently completed a buyout of the Dasa plant at Speyer (IRS, pp. 25–26). The Dasa plant, owned by Dilmer-Benz, specializes in aircraft, space, defence and propulsion systems. Dasa ran into financial difficulty in 1995, and a rationalization plan was developed to try to restore profitability. Dasa wanted to sell the Speyer plant, but could not find a buyer, and therefore considered either closing it down or scaling back operations considerably. An employee buyout plan was considered the best alternative, particularly as the workers, who would be required to make sacrifices, would have a stake in making the plan work. The Speyer plant employed 560 workers and 40 apprentices. Two-thirds of the workers were blue collar, 70-80 per cent were male, and the average age was 35–40. About 95 per cent were members of the metalworkers' union, IG Metall.

The plant became an independent company, Pfaly-Flugyeugwerke GmbH, on 1 January 1997, when it passed to the employees for a symbolic price of DM1. The company retained the former hierarchy, but with a reduced management structure: a three-person team managed the company. The entire workforce was to receive shares of stock in the company, with the same allocation for management and non-management, and allotment to be made on the basis of age and length of service. Dasa provided start-up aid to the new company in the form of land, buildings and equipment, worth DM70 million. The company was also to receive a loan of DM40 million from the State. Dasa also promised to buy the company's aircraft parts at world prices until 2002 to help secure the firm's future in the medium term. The company is intending to expand its product lines in the future and to develop a new customer base.

There were no compulsory redundancies under the buyout, with the necessary workforce reductions coming from voluntary redundancies and early retirement. Cost cutting was achieved by increasing working time from 35 hours to 37.5 hours per week (an extra 30 minutes per day), with no increase in pay. A special agreement was needed from IG Metall for this arrangement, which contravened the working-time provisions of the collective agreement in the metalworking sector. Cost cutting was also achieved through changes to the bonus system and a pay freeze throughout 1997.

Employee buyouts remain relatively uncommon in Germany, and usually only arise from efforts to save a failing company. The only real difference between an employee buyout company and a regular company is that employees hold shares in the new company. Employee buyouts can provide enhanced workers' motivation, effort and commitment to the firm.

In another example of employee ownership, Bell Canada and the Communications, Energy and Paperworkers Union of Canada came to an agreement on setting up a union-supported company to take over some of the utility company's phone-wire repair operation. The newly formed company, Newco, was financed by the Quebec Federation of Labour's Solidarity Fund. The new company will save 800 or more union jobs.

The union decided to form the repair company after the Canadian Radio-Television and Telecommunications Commission declared that single-line customers have the right to hire non-Bell contractors to install or repair phone wiring. Other phone companies in Alberta and British Columbia had been granted similar rulings. Bell Canada agreed to contract out its repair and installation work to the new union-backed company. Bell has also offered a buyout package to its workers who join Newco.

Using a slightly different approach, Telecom Italia, the major Italian tele-communications company, was able to minimize lay-offs by introducing franchising as an alternative to redundancy. Employees faced with redundancy were given the opportunity to open a franchise shop selling Telecom products. The company currently has roughly 150 directly run shops, but plans to close around 45 of these and open 300 new franchise shops run by former Telecom employees, with two workers per franchise. Former Telecom employees taking up franchises are entitled to receive a lump sum equivalent to four months' previous pay, and a week of training and advice on obtaining the necessary commercial licences.

Shorter hours to save jobs

Another means of averting or at least minimizing lay-offs is to introduce flexible working-time arrangements. Under this type of scenario, all workers at the enterprise agree to a percentage reduction in working hours, accompanied by certain reductions in pay, rather than laying off an equal percentage of workers. Such an agreement was reached in 1996 at Fiorucci, a well-known food-processing company in Italy. Fiorucci was planning to reduce its workforce, but following substantial strike action it agreed with the union to promote "vertical" part-time work in order to avoid lay-offs. According to the agreement, workers at all levels of the enterprise can voluntarily request that their full-time employ-ment contracts be converted into part-time contracts, with the reduction in hours calculated on a yearly, rather than a weekly basis. Working hours would be concentrated during the six months from July to December, when demand for the company's product is greatest.

A reduction in working time was also negotiated between Ford Motor Company and the Metal Workers of São Bernardo do Campo, Brazil, in 1996. Faced with an intense fall in demand, the parties agreed to establish a four-day working week with three rest-days in order to save jobs. If the economic situation of the company were reversed in the following year, the agreement would contemplate a return to the traditional five-day working week.

A similar approach to reducing working hours in order to save jobs was reached in Canada. The retail sector there has experienced a downturn, which is tied to the overall sluggishness of the economy. Chain grocery stores, for example, have begun consolidating their operations and closing down shops in various locations. Ordinarily, these store closures would result in lay-offs. However, to minimize the effects of downsizing, the United Food and Commercial Workers Union (UFCW) consented to converting positions from full time to part time in order to avoid lay-offs. The parties have negotiated agreements enabling full-time workers to move to another store location and continue working on a part-time basis. Although this is not a long-term solution, it does give workers the opportunity to remain with the same company, where they can maintain their seniority, continue to accrue pension credits and retain their benefits.

Compensation cuts or freezes for minimizing lay-offs

In some countries, such as India, alternatives to plant closures are regulated by law, rather than through collective bargaining. The following case provides a contrast to the kinds of flexible and innovative approaches to averting lay-offs described above that were achieved through the collective bargaining process.

In India, the Sick Industrial Companies Act of 1985 identifies a number of strict clauses which workers must agree to in order for the Board of Industrial and Financial Reconstruction to positively consider the workers' plea for revival rather than the closing of a company (India country study). The clauses include the following:

• a wage cut/freeze until the company wipes out its debt;
• a dearness allowance freeze;
• a freeze/deferment of certain employee benefits;
• a freeze/deferment of leave travel concessions;
• a reduction in jobs; and
• an assurance not to resort to industrial action.

These stringent conditions are required of workers as a precondition for the possible revival of companies that are on the brink of liquidation. These assurances must remain in force until the company overcomes its financial problems. Moreover, the state government can even prohibit or curtail the industrial relations rights of workers for up to seven years after the company is declared "sick". For example, at Mandya Paper Mills in Belagula (Karnataka State), a public sector unit, the union agreed to a ten-year wage freeze in January 1996 in order to gain approval of its proposal for the company's revival. The union later gained a reduction to a five-year wage freeze, on the grounds that no other company in India had instituted a ten-year wage freeze. None the less, the Act forced workers to make substantial sacrifices in order to hold on to their jobs – sacrifices that could potentially have been minimized through the bargaining process.

Trade-offs over working time

As previously stated, nearly all trade-offs involve some element of job security and retention. But it is also worth while to examine the trade-offs from the perspective of the type of flexibility being introduced, whether it be changes in working time, employment contracts, wages or work organization.

From the evidence gathered from the country studies, it appears that most trade-offs occur over changes in working time. This may be because such changes readily lend themselves to trade-offs, as both employers and workers can derive benefits from these arrangements. The following reasons may explain the prevalence of trade-offs over working time.

First, changes in working time rarely involve a major overhaul of the way in which an enterprise conducts its business. Although the hours of work may change, with differences in starting and finishing times, for example, jobs often remain the same. Disruption on the job, and the insecurity that such disruption creates, is therefore minimized. Second, deviations from standard working hours are becoming more socially acceptable. With a growing number of businesses operating during the evenings and at weekends, for instance, workers themselves are becoming less tied to the traditional, Monday-to-Friday, 9-5 working week. Third, changes in working time rarely involve a significant change in income. In most cases, the compensation remains the same, but is just distributed differently. Under annualized hours, for example, workers receive a consistent pay cheque throughout the year, regardless of the actual hours worked in a given week, rather than overtime pay one week and standard pay the next. Some workers may even prefer this arrangement because it can bring greater regularity to their household budgeting.

From the employers' perspective, changes in working time can generate major cost savings, either by reducing overtime costs or by making more efficient use of capital equipment, and all with little investment in effort or resources. Any trade-offs that employers strike with their workers over working time are often well worth the price. Adjusting working hours enables the enterprise to conform better to fluctuating demands – without having to incur overtime expenses. Since many enterprises have a natural ebb and flow in their business cycles, where workloads are high at certain periods and fall off at others, employers prefer the flexibility of adjusting working hours to meet these changes.

Annualized hours for shorter working time

The primary tactic employers are pushing regarding working-time flexibility is to average weekly working hours over longer periods – anywhere from two weeks to an entire year. Under an annualized hours scheme, for example, workers are compensated according to the total number of hours worked over the course of a year, rather than on a weekly basis; during peak periods, they may be expected to put in a 60-hour week, which may be reduced to 20 hours per week during slack periods. The employer avoids overtime premiums as long as total hours remain below a pre-set level. The trade-off for workers typically comes in the form of reduced working hours and/or an increase in hourly wages, which workers accept as compensation for the growing instability of their working week.

Several companies in the United Kingdom adopted annualized hours as part of their quality- and performance-driven packages in the late 1980s and early 1990s. Plant closures and redundancies were occurring throughout the country during this time, and annualized hours was one means of saving costs – by eliminating the need for overtime pay – and thereby restoring competitiveness and ensuring employment security. Annualized hours became particularly popular in industries with variable and unpredictable demand, and where weekend shifts had been added to the regular working week.

At a Peugeot plant based in the United Kingdom, for instance, the workforce accepted a move to annualized hours in exchange for an increase in leave entitlement to seven weeks, improvements in the pension scheme, a reduction in annual working time by 20 hours, and an above-inflation pay increase of 5 per cent. The new working arrangement involves a four-day work-week and longer shifts. Working time can vary between 30 and 48 hours per week, enabling seven-day manufacturing when necessary. The British motor vehicle unions were initially opposed to the scheme because they felt it would involve compulsory overtime, whereas overtime had previously been voluntary. They overcame their objections when they were able to put together a good financial package and reduced working hours for their members. The company believes that the new working-time arrangements will allow for an 80 per cent increase in production capacity without the huge capital investments normally associated with this kind of expansion.

Another example of an annualized hours agreement in the United Kingdom was reached with British Gypsum, a plasterboard company. The company wanted to move to this system as a way of improving its competitiveness against companies using cheaper imports. The annualized hours system was introduced in 1989 along with a new team-based flexible working system. The 41-hour working week was converted into 1,871.2 annual hours, and 208 credit hours were added to cover sickness, absence, training and any sudden increases in demand without resorting to overtime. If worked, these extra 208 hours would not warrant any additional pay, but neither would there be a deduction if they were not worked. Since the plan has been implemented, nothing close to the 208 hours has been called for, so the result has been an employee benefit of reduced working time.

Flexible hours for added time off

A similar approach to reducing overtime costs is to grant workers compensatory time off in lieu of overtime pay. Overtime hours can be put into an "hours bank," which employees can later draw upon when the workload subsides. As with annualized hours schemes, workers have an inducement to accept the compensatory time off because the overall hours worked during the year typically drop.

Such was the case in the 1995 national agreement in the Italian textile industry. The objective was to limit overtime and short-time compensation, while giving firms the flexibility to vary working hours depending on periods of demand. According to the terms of the agreement, employees may work up to 96 hours of overtime per year, with a maximum of 48 hours of work in any given week. Rather than paying workers a premium for this overtime work, the employer will grant them time off (on a one-for-one basis) during periods of less intensive product demand. Workers receive their regular weekly pay, during both overtime and short weeks. In cases of excessive overtime, above the annual 96-hour contractual limit, workers will be paid a premium of 12 per cent for the first 48 hours and 15 per cent for the next 48 hours. The agreement also introduces the possibility of extending plant utilization to six days per week. Those working the six-day week receive a reduction in weekly working time of 12 hours.

In another example, General Motors Brazil and the metallurgy trade union of São Caetano do Sul recently established a flexible working week, ranging from 33 to 46 hours. Under the agreement, workers are guaranteed a minimum payment for 42 hours per week, even if they actually work fewer hours. Thus they have the security of receiving a consistent pay cheque, even if the working hours vary from week to week. The hours paid but not worked constitute a "debit" and are compensated quarterly by the "credits" of excess hours worked. Overall, workers end up working fewer than 42 hours per week on average – and so come out ahead.

Shift work for higher wages

Rather than strictly focusing on labour cost-cutting measures, a number of firms are seeking ways to improve productivity and efficiency as a means of increasing competitiveness. For example, manufacturing companies are finding that they can expand their productivity by moving towards continuous production. Given the high capital costs involved in a manufacturing operation, a firm can make better use of its investments by running the operation 24 hours a day, or seven days a week.

This kind of continuous production, however, necessitates a change in working time away from standard hours to shift work. For most workers, shift work is viewed as highly undesirable; hence, employers have to offer positive inducements to persuade them to agree to these kinds of arrangements. Those working the night shift, for example, often receive a salary differential to compensate for the unsocial hours. In other cases, shiftworkers receive a reduction in their weekly hours without a corresponding reduction in pay.

Bonfiglioli, a metalworking company based in Bologna, Italy, recently signed a major accord introducing shift work. Work is divided among three rotating shifts, varying from 30 to 35 hours per week, but compensation is retained at the previous level based on a 40-hour week. Those working the day and evening shifts will have a 35-hour week, while those on the overnight shift will have a 30-hour week. Saturday will be considered a normal working day, with each person working at least one Saturday per month. In this case, the reduced working week was enough to convince workers to agree to non-standard working hours.

The construction industry in Australia has also introduced trade-offs regarding flexible working time in exchange for above-average wage increases. For example, the branch agreement in the construction industry for 1996 includes provisions averaging working hours and introducing 12-hour shift arrangements. In exchange, workers have been able to secure annual pay increases ranging from 10 to 15 per cent.

Improved attendance for shorter hours

There are also instances where companies have introduced shorter working weeks with the aim of reducing workers' stress, which in turn would lead to a reduction in absenteeism, sick leave, and turnover. This approach has been particularly popular among Swedish employers. At Volvo, for example, some of the motor manufacturer's departments introduced a scheme of 6.4-hour days four days a week, and 8 hours the fifth day, with no reduction in pay. The main goal of the shorter hours was to reduce the high turnover rates in the assembly department by improving working conditions. Under the new arrangements, the company has reported decreased sick leave and lower turnover, which will enable it to save millions on recruitment costs.

Trade-offs over workers' lifestyles

As mentioned earlier, work-related flexibility is usually introduced at the employers' initiative. There are occasions, however, where workers have been the ones pushing for flexibility to better accommodate their lifestyles. The changing face of the workforce, particularly the growing number of women workers, has meant that rigid notions of working time and employment contracts no longer meet the needs of all workers. As a result, workers too wish for greater flexibility on the job so as to regain control over their busy lives.

Given the increase in female labour force participation the world over, there has been a growing demand for greater flexibility in working time and employment contracts so that workers are better able to combine their work and family responsibilities. In families where both partners are working, shorter or more flexible working hours are often preferable for one, if not both of them. In Europe, for example, 31 per cent of women and 5 per cent of men worked part time in 1995 – an indication that some workers, women in particular, are receptive to more flexible work arrangements. The following are some examples of trade-offs reached to help achieve a better balance between work and family.

Flexible hours for shorter hours

The Netherlands has the highest share of part-time work in total employment of all OECD countries, at 37.4 per cent in 1995. Although some workers may be classified as involuntary part-timers, the country study notes that the growth in part-time employment in the Netherlands is primarily supply driven. This, it is claimed, is stimulated by changes in cultural impediments and a reduction in prejudice towards atypical work arrangements, as increasing proportions of Dutch men and women wish to reduce working hours while maintaining the same hourly rate of pay.

To meet workers' demands for more leisure time, as well as employers' demands for greater working-time flexibility, several recent agreements in the Netherlands have successfully combined flexibility and shorter working hours. In some cases, workers are only required to work four days per week, but they are expected to work in the evenings and/or on Saturdays as part of their regular working week. In other cases, an enterprise can vary the normal working hours from week to week in exchange for lowering the average number of weekly hours. At Nobel Nederland, for example, the working week can range from 32 to 45 hours, provided that the average throughout the year does not exceed 36 hours. Similarly, at Koninklijke PTT Nederland, the normal working week can vary between 30 and 45 hours, as long as the weekly average remains below 37 hours.

Part-time work for more family time

Work and family concerns have also played a role in the switch to more flexible employment contracts. Although many workers prefer the security of a stable, full-time job, a significant number of workers – particularly women – are willing to enter into more tenuous employment contracts so that they have more time to devote to their family caretaking responsibilities. According to a recent employment survey conducted in Ireland, for example, the majority of part-time workers described themselves as part time, rather than underemployed, indicating that they work part time by choice, and not because they were unable to secure full-time employment.

Even where workers voluntarily accept part-time employment, there are often still trade-offs involved. For example, part-time workers have begun demanding wages and benefits comparable to their full-time counterparts to ensure that they are not treated as second-class citizens. In some countries, such as Germany, federal law provides these protections to part-time workers. In others, such as the United States, part-time worker issues have to be resolved through bargaining. This is why most contracts negotiated by the AFSCME, America's largest public sector union, call for wage parity and pro-rated fringe benefits for part-time workers.

New, more flexible work arrangements are also evolving to accommodate an increasingly mobile and dispersed workforce. For example, there are situations where workers may prefer to work longer hours over a period of days in exchange for having several days off in a row. These kinds of arrangements are often favourable to workers travelling long distances to reach their place of employment. Some workers would prefer to avoid daily commuting entirely, opting instead to work from their homes. A combination of technology and flexibility has made it possible for workers to spend less time getting to work and more time pursuing other interests, as described below.

Compressed schedules for greater leave time

The construction and mechanical industries in Norway have begun experimenting with compressed working weeks as a means of accommodating a dispersed workforce. Many workers employed in these industries do not live in the same area in which they work, as companies recruit throughout the Nordic region. To minimize commuting times, some enterprises have initiated a system of working 12 hours a day for 12 consecutive days, followed by nine days off. The unions have supported these arrangements because they benefit workers who must travel long distances to get to the job site.

Norway's mechanical industry, for example, has introduced "offshore" shifts, where working time is reduced from 37.5 hours to 30 hours per week. The working week begins on Thursday, with 3 days of 10 hours per day, then Sunday off and another 3 days of 10 hours. The worker then has a week off, and is free to return home. The monthly salary reflects a 37.5 hour working week, even though only

30 hours are worked. In order to make up the loss in working time, additional workers had to be recruited. But the factory was able to increase its operation time from 37.5 hours to 60 hours per week, which more than compensated for the hourly wage increase and the hiring of additional staff. It should be noted, however, that wage costs represent a relatively small portion of the employer's total costs, which facilitated the move to shorter hours at the same rate of pay.

Telecommuting for avoiding relocation

Technological advances have also made it possible for people to work at home, while keeping in constant contact with the traditional workplace. This phenomenon has become known as "teleworking" or "telecommuting". Employees either work from their homes or at a remote worksite, and are linked to the enterprise through computers, telephone lines and fax machines. They benefit by avoiding the daily commute to the office, and employers benefit by saving on office space. Telecommuting has not yet become widespread, but it has proven highly advantageous for those workers who either cannot or prefer not to leave their homes.

Telecom Italia has built upon the theme of remote working and mobility to contend with overstaffing in some geographical areas and understaffing in others, without having to physically move workers from one location to another. Instead, workers were able to remain in the same place, but certain telephone operator services were provided at long distance. On a voluntary basis, 200 directory information operators were given the opportunity to work half time and at home for at least three years. The company installs all the necessary equipment and pays the power bills, and the agreement states specifically that the teleworker remains part of the company. Workers have benefited by not having to uproot their homes and families in order to keep their jobs.

Trade-offs in other areas

The country studies indicated that trade-offs were far less prevalent in the other areas examined, namely employment contracts, wages and work organization. This may be because these subjects tend to be more controversial, and thus trade-offs are more difficult to achieve.

Employment contracts are the next most common area in which quid pro quos are found, although their incidence is far less frequent than working-time trade-offs – probably because changes in employment contracts typically involve much greater risk for workers than changes in working time. A move to contingent work means a loss of job security. Temporary and contract workers have no assurance that their jobs will continue beyond a specific period, and they are usually excluded from basic employee benefits such as pension plans. Most workers are unwilling to accept this degree of risk, even if the employer offers attractive benefits in return.

It is also important to point out that most trade-offs over employment contracts have been for the benefit of the core staff. In other words, unions have agreed to the introduction of more temporary workers in order to provide greater job security for permanent workers, as in the example at Agco in the United Kingdom mentioned earlier. In most countries, contingent workers have very little trade union representation because their temporary nature makes them difficult to organize and maintain among the union ranks. But as the number of contingent workers begins to rise, and these workers gain in size and strength, the frequency of trade-offs over employment contracts will no doubt grow.

Trade-offs over wage flexibility are also infrequent, mainly because workers are often quite reluctant to accept changes that will directly affect their pay cheques. They are particularly concerned about receiving a secure, regular income in order to pay their bills and provide for their families. Consequently, workers view changes in compensation as quite risky. Not surprisingly, most examples of trade-offs over wages have only come about as an alternative to lay-offs. Workers are willing to accept changes, such as wage cuts or wage moderation only as the last resort for holding on to their jobs. At the same time, many employers have found that introducing more flexible compensation systems is quite a complex task and can prove difficult to implement. Some have even abandoned the practice after a short trial period, finding that wage flexibility can create more problems than it solves.

Finally, the country studies provided almost no evidence of trade-offs being reached over changes in work organization. It is not clear why this is so, but several hypotheses can be offered.

One is that flexibility in work organization often brings benefits to workers as well as managers, thus obviating the need for trade-offs. Changes often arise in an attempt to improve productivity and competitiveness through the proliferation of teamwork, multi-skilling and other aspects of a so-called "high-performance" work organization. This involves the introduction of considerable flexibility, moving away from the notion that each worker performs a single, discrete task to one in which workers perform a variety of functions and have considerable autonomy over their jobs. High-performance work organizations also recognize the value of workers' input into the firm's decision-making process; thus workers' ideas and opinions are given serious consideration.

Various studies have shown that greater flexibility in work organization lends itself to higher productivity and greater efficiency within the enterprise. This focus on enhancing productivity through reorganizing work, rather than cutting labour costs, has become known as the "high road" to competitiveness. Employers in industrialized countries, where wage costs are quite high relative to those in developing countries, are particularly keen to pursue this kind of approach.

In a multi-skilled, teamwork environment, a "win-win" situation can emerge. Workers may gain more interesting and fulfilling jobs, where their opinions are solicited and valued. In some cases, unions have even been successful in reclassifying newly restructured jobs at a higher pay level. Firms, on the other hand, gain higher levels of productivity and efficiency. Under these circumstances, the trade-offs, if they exist, are more subtle than those discussed above.

A contrary argument is that flexibilization of work organization lends itself to workers' exploitation, leaving no room for trade-offs. Under a restructured work environment, workers may be given more complex tasks and greater responsibility, without any corresponding increases in pay or status. Furthermore, restructuring often goes hand in hand with downsizing, so that the remaining workers are required to do the same amount of work previously done by a much larger staff. Because of the potential perils of changes in work organization, workers may be reluctant to join with employers to create a restructured work environment. Since changes often require some involvement by the workers in order to be implemented, such as participation in training courses, it is difficult to achieve them without the workers' cooperation. Similar problems do not arise with flexibility in working time, for example, which can usually be directly implemented without much input from workers.

Shorter hours to expand employment

As discussed above, efforts to expand employment are usually dealt with at higher levels of bargaining. However, there are notable instances where individual enterprises have sought ways to expand employment by introducing greater flexibility in working time or employment contracts. The most common practice is for firms to introduce shorter hours in order to spread employment.

In the municipality of Vaxjo, Sweden, for example, employees were offered shorter hours if they accepted a lower salary increase. The working time was reduced by 11 per cent, from 40 to 35 hours per week. Of the 5,600 employees presented with the offer, 125 accepted. These workers will continue to get paid for an 8-hour day, and a 40-hour week, but they will have to forgo the planned wage increase – which amounted to about 10 per cent of the wage budget. The motivation for management to participate in the project was to reduce unemployment. To that end, the reduction in working hours produced 10 to 15 new jobs. This plan is closely related to the priority given to full employment by the Swedish Government.

Another example of reducing working hours as a way to expand employment comes from Canada. The Canadian Autoworkers (CAW) union negotiated a series of provisions dealing with shorter working time during its 1993 round of bargaining with the big three motor manufacturers. The standard working hours at the Chrysler Windsor minivan plant, for example, were reduced from 8 to 7.5 hours per day, without any loss of pay. The agreement also included introducing a third shift, an increase and restructuring of paid time off, and a phased-in retirement plan. Together these provisions were expected to create 800 new jobs at the plant.

The CAW also negotiated four-day weekends three times a year at Ford and Chrysler, and four times a year at General Motors. The Ford contract even contained a provision calling for mandatory vacations, to make sure that workers took time off the job. Workers at each of the three companies also received a new mandatory week off. CAW estimates that the combined effect of all of these provisions to reduce working time will create or save up to 5,000 union jobs in the motor industry.

In France, a series of agreements was reached at the enterprise level in the mid-nineties in line with the Government's directive on maintaining employment levels. With unemployment in double figures, some French employers have agreed to share responsibility to deal with this problem. For instance, GAN Assurances, an insurance group with 9,300 employees, reached an agreement on employment and working time. Under the accord, employees may switch to a wide range of part-time work, including two forms of "school" part-time working. The options range from employees' taking time off that corresponds with school holidays, to working part time for study purposes, or to working 60 per cent as part of a job-share arrangement. As long as voluntary part-timers comprise at least 15 per cent of the workforce, employees have the unconditional right to return to full-time status. As an inducement for accepting part-time hours, workers would be paid higher wages – 57.5 per cent for half-time work or 66 per cent for the 60 per cent job sharing – or enhanced pensions.

The deal was expected to create 200 jobs, 100 of which would be filled by young people on work/training contracts. Those under the age of 26 would be recruited on training contracts, where they would study to achieve a higher technical certificate in insurance while receiving internal training on products and procedures. GAN promised to hire these young workers at the end of their training contracts, as long as their performance was satisfactory and the company's economic situation permitted it.

The above examples from Sweden, Canada and France demonstrate the role that individual employers and unions can play in improving the job prospects of unemployed workers. Although national policy may have supported their actions to expand employment, it was left to collective bargaining at the enterprise level to follow through the proposed innovations.

Concluding remarks

Since the introduction of flexibility into the labour market typically entails sacrifices on the part of workers – in terms of stability of employment or modification of their lifestyles – success is possible only if workers consent to the changes. Such consent is best obtained through trade-offs in which workers' concessions are met with reciprocal concessions by employers. The evidence supplied in this chapter supports the argument that the collective bargaining process provides the best forum for achieving workable trade-offs in the area of flexibility because, in essence, bargaining is primarily about quid pro quos. The give-and-take of bargaining induces each side to compromise on its starting position in an effort to reach an acceptable outcome. By enabling workers and management to arrive jointly at a workable solution – rather than having the employer unilaterally decide what is best for the organization – collective bargaining can instill in workers a sense of commitment to the change process and build trust, leading to a better working relationship on both sides.

CONCLUSION

Major changes are taking place in all four aspects of the labour market addressed in this book, namely employment relationships, wages, working time and work organization. These changes are aimed at removing what employers, policy makers and an increasing number of workers and their trade unions regard as rigidities in regulating or operating the labour market. The removal of such rigidities is expected to enhance the competitiveness of the enterprise or national economy and reduce unemployment.

Although there is today wide consensus among the social partners that more flexibility is needed in the labour market, there is considerable divergence between the views of employers and workers as to the desirability of particular forms of flexibility, as well as the ways in which they are to be introduced. While employers are generally in favour of greater flexibility in all four aspects of the labour market studied, workers' views vary with the specific types of labour market flexibility at issue, as well as the country concerned. The particular forms of flexibility introduced differ according to such factors as the specific product market conditions facing the enterprise and the industry, the ideological orientation of a particular government, and the industrial relations climate prevailing in the enterprise, industry or country.

Flexibility in employment, with the exception of part-time employment, is generally regarded with great suspicion by workers. In particular, they strongly oppose relaxing control over dismissals, although, where temporary employment is widespread, trade unions may acquiesce to relaxing restrictions on dismissals in return for the employers' commitment to converting temporary employment to employment for an indefinite duration – as was the case in the central agreement entered into in Spain in 1997 between the central employers' and workers' organizations. A similar situation exists in the Netherlands, where the social partners have made an effort to flexibilize individual employment relationships, while offering a reasonable degree of protection and stability to the workers who are party to such relationships. While there has undoubtedly been a significant increase in the number of employees working under flexible contracts of employment, there is no unanimity, even among employers, about the advantages of flexible employment. Some flexible forms of employment, for example temporary employment, tend to increase the costs of training workers and lead to lower commitment and skill levels among workers. At a time of global competition and the growing importance of quality as a factor of competitiveness, this is a serious drawback, and employers are becoming increasingly aware of this fact. Accordingly, when new legislation widens the opportunity for employers to resort to flexible employment – by removing prior restrictions, for example – this does not always give rise to the spread of non-standard employment. Employers may still prefer to maintain standard (permanent) employment, as seems to have been the case in New Zealand after the introduction of the Employment Contracts Act of 1991 (Brosnan and Walsh, 1996, cited in the New Zealand country study).

From the viewpoint of the effectiveness of union action in protecting the interests of workers in flexible employment, or contingent workers, there is a notable difference between unions operating in decentralized industrial relations (as in the United States and Japan) and those in centralized industrial relations (as in continental Europe). Enterprise unions in decentralized industrial relations often face legal and other constraints in representing contingent workers; thus their organizational drives generally focus on workers in standard employment. When they seek to improve employment conditions for contingent workers, they often do so by converting contingent employment into full-time, permanent employment, although there are some notable examples of unions in decentralized industrial relations systems making considerable efforts to organize contingent workers. On the other hand, unions in centralized industrial relations systems – which tend to encompass a much broader membership, drawn from various segments of the working population – typically have fewer cultural impediments or organizational difficulties. They tend to be more interested in improving conditions for contingent workers as such, and amplify the advantages which flexible employment can give to these workers. Behind these differences lie two fundamentally different concepts of trade unions, one as institutions representing their members, and another as institutions representing the working class in society as a whole.

Pay structure and procedures for determining pay have also undergone notable changes. An important aspect of pay flexibility in the present context concerns the level at which pay bargaining should be conducted. Policy makers and social partners widely perceive bargaining at the enterprise level as more flexible than bargaining at a higher level, and as more conducive to better economic performance. Consequently, there has been a clear trend over the past decade towards decentralizing wage bargaining, although sectoral and central wage bargaining continue to play an important role in many Western European countries, at least in so far as they establish a framework for enterprise bargaining. In those countries where the union structure has traditionally been centralized, this trend towards decentralization has subjected unions to pressures for organizational and functional change.

However, whether or not decentralization actually leads to better economic performance is a subject of considerable controversy. One extreme view regards central bargaining as a form of intervention by non-market institutions in the free play of market forces, which is harmful to economic performance. A radically opposite view considers centralized bargaining to be beneficial to economic performance because of its ability to overcome various market failures. Research evidence has presented a more complex picture, ranging from a so-called "U-shaped relationship" between a country's economic performance and the level of collective bargaining – meaning that both highly centralized and decentralized bargaining perform better than intermediate forms of bargaining (Calmfors and Driffel, 1988) – to relationships in which the effectiveness of coordinating wage bargaining – rather than centralized bargaining as such – is an important variable affecting economic performance (Traxler and Kittel, 1997; Nickell, 1997; Soskice, 1990). Recent trends observed in many countries in this study, namely trends towards decentralization without the demise of bargaining at the central level, are therefore consistent with recent research evidence, and reinforce our belief that enterprise-level bargaining, when guided by the principles of mutual gains and supported by effective social dialogue at the central level, is conducive to high levels of economic efficiency.

Innovations have also been introduced into working-time arrangements and work organization at an accelerating pace during the past decade or so, with a view to enhancing "internal numerical flexibility" and "functional flexibility" respectively. Workers' reactions to enhanced flexibility in these areas have been complex. Greater flexibility in working-time arrangements often implies a reduction in take-home pay, as overtime tends to be integrated into flexibilized normal working hours. In addition, flexible hours frequently involve more or less compulsory night or weekend work. Despite these disadvantages, however, workers are not always hostile to working-time flexibility, as it may give them new possibilities for enjoying their private or family life, especially where they can participate in scheduling flexible working time. On the other hand, workers with family responsibilities that restrict them to regular, limited working hours will not be in a position to take up more flexible schedules, and this may in turn restrict their employment opportunities. This ambiguity in workers' attitudes towards flexible working time has created some difficulties for unions, which have traditionally sought to improve standardized employment conditions equally for all their members. In some innovative cases, the management of flexible working time has been entrusted to teams of workers, the team being held responsible for the accomplishment, on schedule, of work assignments. In such cases, some of the protective functions of trade unions are transferred to work teams, creating a danger of their undermining trade union functions.

All in all, labour market flexibility has had the main objective of enhancing competitiveness in the context of globalized markets. It has therefore entailed many sacrifices on the part of the workers, although some forms of flexibility have been in line with workers' aspirations. In most cases, however, flexibility has meant less employment security, less income security, and a continuous adjustment to new, often more uncomfortable working conditions, which workers have accepted in order to avoid the worst scenario (i.e. unemployment due to plant closures or to a decline in the competitiveness of the national economy). It is therefore clear that the introduction of flexibility can be smoothly implemented only if workers are associated with the process, and their views are duly taken into account in selecting the forms of flexibility to be introduced and determining the ways in which they should be introduced. The critical element for the success of such association is the quality of the relationship between the employers and employees. Mutual trust and loyalty, as well as the intensity of consultation between the two parties, define the relationship: collective bargaining, in the broadest sense of the term, can be an appropriate means of enhancing the quality of the employer-employee relationship, as it legitimizes the decisions taken as well as the process of decision-making. In the absence of a representative voice, there is a danger that workers' views are either not expressed, for fear of antagonizing managers, or are ignored (United Kingdom country study).

The same observation also applies to macroeconomic and social policy making. Consultation among governments, and employers' and workers' organizations, gives legitimacy to policies, and increases the likelihood of the sacrifices involved being accepted by employers and workers. Despite the general decline observed today in union density, trade unions remain the only institutions capable of representing the voice of those who are the primary producers of economic wealth. This is why the governments of many countries still frequently resort to tripartite consultations and negotiations, in particular when faced with the need to take drastic measures for flexibilizing the labour market. The signing, in February 1998, of a tripartite agreement on the reform of the labour market in the Republic of Korea – a country where there was previously no tradition of social dialogue – in the wake of the serious financial crisis in Asia, illustrates the decisive advantages of associating workers' and employers' organizations in formulating policies that require sacrifices from all the actors in the economic life of the country.

However, the process of collective bargaining must adapt itself to the requirements of flexibility. The discussions in the preceding chapters enable us to draw conclusions with some policy implications:

- Collective bargaining cannot be a highly adversarial process if it is to be an instrument for developing high-trust relationships between management and individual employees – a prerequisite for maximizing the employees' commitment to continuous improvement. Several cases of flexibility bargaining, reviewed in this book, confirm this simple, common-sense truth: a relationship of trust enables the implementation of flexibility measures that are beneficial to both parties in the long term but require considerable short-term sacrifices from workers.
- A collective bargaining process that integrates elements of joint problem solving tends to be more successful as an instrument for introducing labour market flexibility than a collective bargaining process that merely establishes rights and procedures. Flexibility is about adaptability to the changing conditions of an increasingly competitive and technologically advanced global market. Therefore, the process of collective bargaining itself will have to become more flexible and cooperative in order to facilitate the joint search for ways of pursuing continuous improvement.
- Collective bargaining tends to be more effective in enhancing labour market flexibility when decentralized bargaining is supported by mechanisms of coordination at a higher level. These mechanisms of coordination may be either formal, and effective, centralized bargaining or informal coordination among different enterprises or industries. Governments can play an important role in promoting such coordination.

Collective bargaining can be instrumental in labour market flexibility only if it can function as an effective means of industrial regulation. If, for example, bargaining is conducted without the mutual recognition of labour and management as equal partners, it will not achieve an outcome acceptable to both sides. As the successful introduction of labour market flexibility requires the whole-hearted support of the workers involved, collective bargaining in which one side holds the upper hand and imposes changes without offering reciprocal benefits cannot be an effective means of introducing flexibility. However, the absence of a balance of power between the parties is more the rule than the exception in collective bargaining in many countries, particularly in the developing world. Under these circumstances, flexibility bargaining sometimes results only in the acknowledgement of managerial prerogatives in introducing flexibility, as often seems to be the case with enterprise-level flexibility agreements in India (India country study). Thus, the effectiveness of collective bargaining as an instrument for labour market flexibility depends largely on the strength of workers' organizations.

The State can also play an important role in strengthening trade unions, and promoting flexibility bargaining. Laws favouring, or at least not impeding, the affiliation of workers to trade unions and the recognition of trade unions for the purposes of collective bargaining are clearly a prerequisite for making collective bargaining a major force in negotiating flexibility. Moreover, legal rules can restrict or open up options available to the social partners, and often play a key role in determining whether a synergy can develop between legislation and collective bargaining, or whether a stalemate will emerge and persist. If legislation greatly restricts the terms and conditions that can be negotiated, the role which collective bargaining can play in introducing flexibility will be very limited. On the other hand, if legislation encourages the social partners to implement provisions through agreements among them, the role of collective bargaining in relation to flexibility will increase.

Admittedly, collective bargaining is not the only means of introducing labour market flexibility – particularly since the flexibilization process often requires a change of legislation. However, as this study shows, such legislative changes can be – and often are – the outcome of a tripartite consultation or negotiation process ("negotiated legislation"). In comparison with legislation, collective bargaining has the advantage of being a flexible instrument allowing those affected by the proposed changes to determine the types of changes, as well as the pace and the process of their introduction. In comparison with employers' unilateral decisions or individual contracts of employment, collective bargaining has the advantage of lending legitimacy to decisions in workers' minds, as the process enables workers, through their representatives, to express their views independently of employers. As a means of introducing labour market flexibility, only collective bargaining can offer these two advantages together.

BIBLIOGRAPHY

Araki, T. 1997. "Changing Japanese labor law in light of deregulation drives: A comparative analysis", in *Japanese Labor Bulletin* (Tokyo), Vol. 36, No. 5, May.

Atkinson, J. 1984. "Manpower strategies for flexible organisations", in *Personnel Management* (London), 28–31 Aug.

Belous, R.S. 1989. *The contingent economy: The growth of the temporary, part-time and subcontracted workforce* (Washington, DC, National Planning Association).

Berggren, C. 1992. *Alternatives to lean production* (Ithaca, New York, ILR Press).

Betten, L. 1995. *The employment contract in transforming labour relations* (The Hague, Kluwer Law International).

Blackman, C. 1997. *Country report for Barbados on collective bargaining and flexibility* (unpublished).

Bronstein, A. 1997. "Labour reform in Latin America: Between state protection and flexibility", in *International Labour Review* (Geneva, ILO), Vol. 136, No. 1.

Brosnan, P. 1996. "The dynamics of change between standard and non-standard employment", in J. Teicher, (ed.): *Non-standard employment in Australia and New Zealand*, Monograph No. 9 (Melbourne, National Key Center for Industrial Relations).

—; Thornwaite, L. 1994. "Atypical work in Australia: Preliminary results of a Queensland study", in R. Callus and M. Schumacher (eds.): *Current research in industrial relations: Proceedings of the 8th AIRAANZ Conference* (Sydney, Association of Industrial Relations Academics of Australia and New Zealand).

—; Walsh, P. 1996. *Plus ça change ... : The Employment Contracts Act and non-standard employment in New Zealand*, 1991–1995, Working Paper 4/96 (Wellington, Industrial Relations Centre, Victoria University).

Browne, J. 1997. "The juridification of the employment relationship: Implications and issues", in F. Meenan (ed.): *Legal perspectives – The juridification of the employment relationship,* Official Proceedings of the Fifth IIRA European Regional Congress, Dublin, Ireland, August 1997 (Dublin, Oak Tree Press).

Burkins, G. 1996. "Temps joining unions", in *Wall Street Journal,* 12 Dec.

Calmfors, L.; Driffel, J. 1988. "Bargaining structure, corporatism and macroeconomic performance", in *Economic Policy* (Cambridge), No. 5, Apr.

Card, D.; Krueger, A. 1995. "Myth and measurement: The new economics of the minimum wage", in *Industrial and Labor Relations Review* (Ithaca, New York), Vol. 48, No. 4, July.

Clerc, J.-M. (ed.). 1985. *Introduction to working conditions and environment* (Geneva, ILO).

Collins, H. 1997. "The productive disintegration of labour law", in *Industrial Law Journal* (London), Vol. 26, No. 4, Dec.

Cranfield School of Management. 1996. *Working time and contract flexibility in the European Communities* (Cranfield, Bedfordshire).

Crawford, A.; Harbridge, R.; Hince, K. 1996. *Unions and union membership in New Zealand: Annual review for 1995,* Working Paper 2/96 (Wellington, Victoria University).

Dabshek, B. 1994. "The arbitration system since 1967", in S. Bell and B. Head (eds.): *State, economy and public policy* (Melbourne, Oxford University Press).

Däubler, W. 1988. "Deregulierung und Flexibilisierung im Arbeitsrecht", in *WSI-Mitteilungen* (Cologne), 8/1988.

Delsen, L. 1995. *Atypical employment: An international perspective; Causes, consequences and policy* (Gröningen, Wolters-Noordhoff).

de Grip, A.; Hoevenberg, J.; Willems, E. 1997. "Atypical employment in the European Union", in *International Labour Review* (Geneva, ILO), Vol. 136, No. 1.

European Commission (EC). 1996. *Employment in Europe,* DG V (Luxembourg, Office for Official Publications of the European Communities).

Eurostat. 1996. *Labour Force Survey 1990–1995* (Luxembourg, Office for Official Publications of the European Communities).

Flanders, A. 1964. *The Fawley productivity agreements* (London, Faber and Faber).

Freedland, M. 1995. "The role of the contract of employment in modern labour law", in Betten, op. cit.

Fredman, S. 1997. "Labour law in flux: The changing composition of the workforce", in *Industrial Law Journal* (London), Vol. 26, No. 4, Dec.

Gazon, E. 1995. "La décentralisation des négociations collectives dans la métallurgie: Limites et différenciations", in *Travail et Emploi* (Paris), No. 65, Apr.

Ghellab, Y. 1998. *Minimum wage and youth employment*, Action Programme on Youth Employment (Geneva, ILO).

Harbridge, R.; Crawford, A. 1997. "The Employment Contracts Act and collective bargaining patterns: A review of the 1995/96 year", in R. Harbridge, A. Crawford and P. Kiely: *Employment contracts: Bargaining trends and employment law update 1995/96* (Wellington, Industrial Relations Centre, Victoria University).

—; Honeybone, A. 1995. "The Employment Contracts Act and collective bargaining patterns: A review of the 1994/95 year", in R. Harbridge and P. Kiely (eds.): *Employment contracts: Bargaining trends and employment law update 1994/95* (Wellington, Industrial Relations Centre, Victoria University).

—, Honeybone, A. 1996. "External legitimacy of unions: Trends in New Zealand", in *Journal of Labor Research* (Fairfax, Virginia), Vol. 17, No. 3, Summer.

—; Rea, D. 1992. "Collective bargaining and the labour market debate in New Zealand: A review", in *Economic and Labour Relations Review* (Sydney), Vol. 3, No. 1.

Huiskamp, R. 1998. "Diversity of employment relations: Collective bargaining regenerates (in the Netherlands), but does industrial relations theory?", in T. Wilthagen (ed.): *Advancing theory in labour law and industrial relations in a global context* (Amsterdam, North-Holland), pp. 143–150.

Hyman, R. 1998. "Industrial relations in Europe: Crisis or reconstruction", in Wilthagen, op. cit.

Ibsen, F. 1997. "The role of the state in industrial relations in the Nordic countries", in J. Browne (ed.): *The role of the state in industrial relations,* Official Proceedings of the Fifth IIRA European Regional Congress, Dublin, Ireland, August 1997 (Dublin, Oak Tree Press).

ILO. 1988. *Assessing the impact of statutory minimum wages in developing countries: Four country studies* (Geneva), Labour-Management Relations Series No. 67.

—. 1996. *Tripartite consultation at the national level on economic and social policy,* Report VI, International Labour Conference, 83rd Session, Geneva, 1996.

—. 1997. *World Labour Report 1997–98: Industrial relations, democracy and social stability* (Geneva).

Industrial Relations Services (IRS). 1991. "Annualised hours – The concept of the flexible year", in *Employment Trends* (London), No. 488, May.

Industrial Relations Services (IRS). 1994. "Non-standard working under review", ibid., No. 565, Aug.

—. 1997. "Employee buy-out secures future of Dasa plant at Speyer", in *European Industrial Relations* Review (London), No. 282, July.

Institute of Applied Manpower Research. 1996. *Manpower Profile India: Yearbook 1996* (New Delhi).

Jacobi, O.; Hassel, A. 1996. "Does direct participation threaten the 'German Model'?", in I. Regalia and C. Gill (eds.): *The position of the social partners in Europe on direct participation.* Country Studies: Volume II, Working Paper No. WP/96/03/EN (Dublin, European Foundation for the Improvement of Living and Working Conditions).

Kaisergruber, D.; Bernard Brunhes Consultants. 1997. *Négocier la flexibilité: Pratiques en Europe* (Paris, Eds. d'Organisation).

Keller, B.; Soerries, B. 1997. "The new social dialogue: New concepts, first results and future perspectives", in P. Flood et al.: *The European Union and the employment relationship*, Official Proceedings of the Fifth IIRA European Regional Congress, Dublin, Ireland, August 1997 (Dublin, Oak Tree Press).

Lansbury, R.; Kochan, T.; MacDuffie, J. 1997. *After lean production: Evolving employment practices in the world auto industry* (Ithaca, New York, ILR Press).

Locke, R.; Kochan, T.; Piore, M. (eds.). 1995. *Employment relations in a changing world economy* (Cambridge, Massachussetts, MIT Press).

Marsden, D. 1996. "Employment policy implications of new management systems", in *Labour: Review of Labour Economics and Industrial Relations* (Oxford), Vol. 10, No. 1, Spring.

Martin, A. 1995. "The Swedish model: Demise or reconfiguration?", in Locke et al., op. cit.

McAndrew, I. 1992. "The structure of bargains under the Employment Contracts Act", in *New Zealand Journal of Industrial Relations* (Wellington), Vol. 17(3).

Melz, N.; Verma, A. 1995. "Developments in industrial relations and human resource practices in Canada: An update from the 1980s", in Locke et al., op. cit.

Michon, F.; Ramaux, C. 1992. "CDD et intérim: bilan d'une décennie", in *Travail et Emploi* (Paris), No. 52.

Ministère du Travail, France. 1996. *Bilan de l'intéressement et de la participation des salariés aux bénéfices de l'entreprise* (Paris, Direction des Relations de Travail).

Ministry of Labour, Japan. *Monthly Report on the Labour Force Survey* (Tokyo), various issues 1985–96.

Morehead, A., et al.; Australia Department of Workplace Relations and Small Business. 1997. *Changes at work: The 1995 Australian Workplace Industrial Relations Survey* (Melbourne, Longman).

Mückenberger, U. 1989. "Der Wandel des Normalarbeitsverhältnisses unter Bedingungen einer 'Krise der Normalität'", in *Gewerkschaftliche Monatshefte* (Cologne), No. 4.

—. 1992. *National report: Germany*, in Veneziani, op. cit.

Murakami, T. 1995. "Introducing team working: A motor industry case study from Germany", in *Industrial Relations Journal* (Oxford), Vol. 26, No. 4, Dec.

New Zealand Institute of Economic Research (NZIER). 1996. *A preliminary report on the results of a survey on the Employment Contracts Act* (Wellington), Working Paper 96/7.

Nickell, S. 1997. "Unemployment and labor market rigidities: Europe versus North America", in *Journal of Economic Perspectives* (Nashville, Tennessee), Vol. 11(3), Summer.

Organisation for Economic Co-operation and Development (OECD). 1993, 1996, 1997. *Employment Outlook* (Paris).

—. 1997. *Economic Survey: The United States* (Paris).

Olney, S. 1996. *Unions in a changing world: Problems and prospects in selected industrialized countries* (Geneva, ILO).

O'Reilly, J. 1994. *Banking on flexibility: A comparison of flexible employment in retail banking in Britain and France* (Aldershot, Hampshire, Avebury Press).

Ozaki, M. 1996a. "Labour relations and work organization in industrialized countries", in *International Labour Review* (Geneva, ILO), Vol. 135, No. 1.

—. 1996b. "Direct participation in work organization: A survey of recent international developments", in *Economic and Labour Relations Review* (Sydney, University of New South Wales), Vol. 7, No. 1, June.

Park, D.J.; Park, K.S. 1991. *Trade unions in Korea* (II) (Seoul, Korea Labor Institute).

Park, K.S. 1992. *Skill formation in Korea* (Seoul, Korea Labor Institute).

Rama, M. 1996. *The consequences of doubling the minimum wage: The case of Indonesia* (Washington, DC, The World Bank), Policy Research Working Paper No. 1643.

Robineau, Y. 1997. "Loi et négociation collective – Rapport au Ministre du Travail et des Affaires sociales", in *Liaisons sociales* (Paris), No. 53/97, Part V, 8 July.

Ryan, R. 1992. "Flexibility in the employment practices of northern firms", in *New Zealand Journal of Industrial Relations* (Wellington), Vol. 17, No. 2.

Sako, M. 1997. "Shunto: The role of employer and union coordination at the industry and intersectoral levels", in M. Sako and H. Sato (eds.): *Japanese labour and management in transition: Diversity, flexibility and participation* (London, Routledge).

Sauerwein, quoted in D. Fröhlich and U. Pekruhl. 1995. *Direct participation and organizational change in Europe, Japan and the USA: An analysis of international research evidence* (Dublin, Foundation for the Improvement of Living and Working Conditions), mimeoed document produced under the EPOC project.

Shaheed, Z. 1997. *Negotiating flexibility in the auto industry in South Africa* (Geneva, ILO; unpublished).

Simitis, S. 1997. "Le droit du travail a-t-il encore un avenir?", in *Droit social* (Paris), No. 7–8, July–Aug.

Soskice, D. 1990. "Wage determination: The changing role of institutions in advanced industrialized countries", in *Oxford Review of Economic Policy* (Oxford), Vol. 6, No. 4.

Statistics Canada. *Labour Force* (Ottawa), various issues 1992–95.

Towers Perrin. 1997. *Learning from the past, changing for the future: A research study of pay and reward challenges and changes in Europe* (London).

Traxler, F.; Kittel, B. 1997. *The bargaining structure, its context and performance: A case of global competition among national bargaining systems?* (Vienna, University of Vienna), paper prepared for the Conference on Economic Internationalization and Democracy, Vienna, 14–15 Dec. 1997.

Treu, T. 1992. "Labour flexibility in Europe", in *International Labour Review* (Geneva, ILO), Vol. 131, No. 4–5.

van Peipje, T. 1998. "The usefulness of comparative methods in studying trends in labour law", in Wilthagen, op. cit.

Vaughan-Whitehead, D., et al. 1995. *Workers' financial participation: East-West experiences* (Geneva, ILO), Labour-Management Relations Series No. 80.

Veneziani, B. 1990. "The new labour force", in R. Blanpain (ed.): *Comparative labour law and industrial relations in industrialised market economies* (Kluwer, Deventer, 4th ed).

Veneziani, B. 1992. *Law, collective bargaining and labour flexibility in EC countries* (Rome, Associazione Sindacale per le Aziende Petrolchimiche e Collegate a Participazione Statale/Instituto Poligrafico e Zecca dello Stato).

Vidmar, S. 1997. *Arbeitszeitpolitik und atypische Arbeitszeitgestaltung: Österreich und Schweden in Vergleich* (Vienna; unpublished thesis).

Watson, G. 1994. "The flexible workforce and patterns of working hours in the UK", in *Employment Gazette* (London), Vol. 192, No. 7, July.

Wever, K. 1997. "Unions adding value: Addressing market and social failures in the advanced industrialized countries", in *International Labour Review* (Geneva, ILO), Vol. 136, No. 4.

Wilthagen, T. (ed.): *Advancing theory in labour law and industrial relations in a global context* (Amsterdam, North-Holland).

Windmuller, J.P., et al. 1987. *Collective bargaining in industrialized market economies: A reappraisal* (Geneva, ILO).

Yoon, J.H. 1996. "Employment adjustment and unions' response in Korea", in *Korean Journal of Labor Studies* (Seoul), Vol. 2, No. 1, Aug.